Worship
Sketches
2
Perform

Steven James

MERIWETHER PUBLISHING LTD.
Colorado Springs, Colorado

Meriwether Publishing Ltd., Publisher
PO Box 7710
Colorado Springs, CO 80933-7710

Editor: Rhonda Wray
Typesetting: Sue Trinko
Cover design: Janice Melvin

Library of Congress Cataloging-in-Publication Data

James Steven, 1969-
  Worship sketches 2 perform : a collection of scripts for two actors / Steven James.
      p.   cm.
  Includes indexes
  ISBN 1-56608-068-1 (pbk.)
  1. Drama in public worship. 2. Christian drama, American. I. Title: Worship sketches two perform. II. Title.

BV289.J35 2000
246'.72--dc21   00-050063
                                                        CIP

         3   4   5   03   04   05

*This book is dedicated to my dear wife, Liesl Huhn,
who believed in me, encouraged me, listened to me, loved me,
and brewed me lots of coffee.*

Contents

Acknowledgments

Special thanks to Tracy Radosevic and Keith Young, two storytellers who watered the early seeds of this book; to Jim Fickley, for his encouragement to keep going; to Chris "Topher" Doerr, for developing ideas with me; to Rhonda Lacey and Dr. Dan Earl, for telling me what worked and what didn't; to Dr. John Paul Abner, for keeping things from getting cheesy; to Jose Castillo, for his off-the-wall ideas that were right on target; to The Heartbeat of the Home, for the inspiration for the Evango-pager; to the Griers, for the teaching dilemma; and to the folks at Grace Fellowship Church, for letting these ideas blossom into worship.

Introduction

Nathan paused with his hand on the doorknob.

If he went through with this, it could mean his career. It could even mean his life. He knew what he had to say; he knew he needed to confront his friend. The only problem was, his friend was the king. And he'd been known to lose his temper.

He'd been known to kill.

In fact, that was one of the things Nathan was there to talk to him about. Murder.

So he paused. At least *I* would have paused.

But he didn't turn back.

Nathan opened that door and told King David a story. It wasn't a religious story. It didn't even mention God. Just a story plucked from everyday life. And when David heard it, his anger flared up, just like Nathan had expected.

"The man who did that ought to die!" shouted David, pounding his fist on the armrest of his throne.

"You are the man," said Nathan.

That day, Nathan used a contemporary "slice-of-life" story to expose David's sin. And it worked. David confessed his sin and found God's forgiveness.

When we identify with the characters in a story, the message embedded in the tale hits home in our lives. When we see real people face real struggles and make discoveries about life, we make the same discoveries. We change. We grow. We confess. We receive forgiveness. That's what this drama called life is all about.

Today, thousands of churches around the world use drama in their ministries each week. Most of these churches depend on volunteer actors and directors. They don't have a troupe of professionally trained thespians and a three-million-dollar drama ministry budget. Overworked directors search for sketches, meet with pastors to discuss ideas, and try to get their actors together for regular rehearsals. *Worship Sketches 2 Perform* was written especially with those directors in mind.

What makes this book different from other script collections?

Over the last twenty years more and more churches have decided to explore the use of drama in their ministries. But the sheer number of churches now "doing drama ministry" doesn't guarantee that what they are doing is either good drama or good ministry. As I worked on this book, I tried to address some of the most common problems I've seen:

"Preachy" writing

Good drama explores difficult questions and gets people thinking about the different sides of sensitive issues. Interesting characters are posed with intriguing choices that deliver real consequences. If the audience can see the ending coming, or the writer adds a mini-sermon at the end of the sketch, it loses its effectiveness. If the sketch engages people — both intellectually and emotionally — and opens the door for a deeper understanding, then the presentation is effective. A sermon and a sketch have different goals. A sermon's goal is to clarify and explain. A sketch's goal is to question and explore. When the purpose of either is blurred, the quality of both suffers. The preaching should be done in the sermon, not the sketch. I've aimed for that goal with the sketches in this book.

No time for casting and directing

Too often the quality of dramatic productions in churches suffers because of lack of rehearsal time. Things are done on the fly or at the last minute. The pastor calls the director on Thursday and says, "Could you guys put together a skit for Sunday?" And, since we want to help, we unwittingly say, "Sure." But producing quality theatre takes time, effort, and commitment. So, as servants of the King of Kings, our goal should be to reach the highest level of excellence rather than lower our expectations simply because "it's only for the church." The sketches in this book will help. They're easy to learn, cast, direct, and perform. Each script includes a plot summary, directing tips, Scripture references, possible themes, and more, to make it as easy as possible to use and produce.

Lack of variety

How many sketches have you seen with two people driving a car or sitting in a restaurant? Lots. Any type of drama used week after week will get old and lose its effectiveness. Therefore, this collection includes slice-of-life vignettes, worship readings, dual monologs, narrative pantomime, retold Bible stories and stories for two tellers. This book isn't meant to be the only resource a drama director uses, but rather a small addition to a growing library of sketches and directing resources.

Who is the audience?

God is.

Yes, the congregation is engaged in the drama, but the goal is not to perform for them, but to lead them closer to an intimate relationship with God. You're not putting on a play here. You're participating in a worship service.

That said, within the context of dramatic performance, throughout this book I'll refer to those who are watching the sketch as the audience. It may be a congregation, a Bible study, a Sunday school group, or a men's conference. God is still the one to whom the drama of worship is directed, but those in attendance are joining with the actors as they express their gifts in service and reverence to God.

Do these sketches stand alone, or do they need to be done in a worship service?

When I was in high school, my English teacher told me that a story had a beginning, a middle, and an ending and I remember thinking, "Yeah? So what? Everything does!" A shopping list has a beginning, a middle, and an end, but it's not a story. So does a paragraph describing a pickle, but it's not a story. So does a line drawn on a sheet of paper. So what makes a story a story?

Well, my teacher had the right concept. But his way of describing it was misleading. The beginning of the story is more than just the first event, it's the originating event. The middle is not just the next event, but the problem. And the ending is not just the last event, but the resolution. Rather than having a beginning, a middle, and an ending, a story really has an origin, a muddle, and a resolution.

Every dramatic situation is at least a piece of a story. Some of the sketches in this book contain an originating event, a muddle (or problem), and a solution. They stand alone. But many of them contain only the first two parts — there is no resolution offered. These sketches expose a raw nerve. They leave the audience feeling confronted and uncomfortable. So where does the resolution come from? The sermon.

Sketches that end with conflict are contextual. They need to be placed in a worship situation where the message or sermon addresses, and offers answers to, the struggle brought to life by the sketch.

Can I use more than two people in any of these sketches?

Yes. All of the sketches were written with just two people in mind, but with a little creativity and flexibility, you could add people to the sketches if you felt it would work better with your actors and in your worship setting.

Any suggestions for me as a director?

I suggest that you begin at the ending, by searching through the theme index to find sketches that address situations or topics your pastor will be covering in upcoming messages. Photocopy the theme list and give it to him. Let him highlight the themes he'll be covering in the next couple months. Then read through the sketches with those themes and offer several ideas to him.

Take notes as you read. Think about your actors and write down who might be best suited for each sketch. Some actors work best in comic roles, others in emotive roles, and others work best in the realm of physicality. Look for ways that each of the sketches will work best with your actors and your church.

Not every sketch in this book will work with every audience. You may need to make slight alterations in the language to fit the needs of your church. So jot down blocking ideas and changes (in wording or names) that might make the sketch more appropriate for your congregation.

Read through the sketches with your drama ministry team. Let your actors feel them out and explore the emotions and movement inherent to the sketch. A drama is a way of handing off an idea. That idea moves from the writer to the director, the director to the actors, and the actors to the audience. But rather than becoming more clouded and fuzzy with each person who encounters it, the idea must become more focused and clear. So allow your creative interpretation and the creative interpretation of your actors to affect the tone, flavor and impact of each sketch so that they can hand off a clear and focused idea to the congregation.

Remember that dramatic presentations can be used in various ways. Some sketches work best to set up the sermon by presenting a conflict or posing a legitimate question that the sermon will then address and answer from God's Word. Some of the sketches include the resolution and may work best after the sermon, or embedded in a time of worship.

Enjoy. As servants of the King of the Universe, our role is to present the highest-quality work for his pleasure, honor, and glory. Let's do that with good drama and good ministry.

NOTES: For the purpose of brevity, throughout this book I will refer to "actors" in the general sense — meaning both male (actors) and female (actresses).

The numerals running vertically down the left margin of each page of dialog are for the convenience of the director. By using them, he/she may easily direct attention to a specific passage.

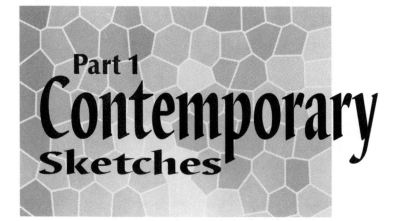

Part 1
Contemporary
Sketches

This first section contains sketches with realistic people in contemporary situations. Remember Nathan's story? About everyday events? That's what these sketches are like.

Not only did Nathan use this type of story, Jesus used it, too. In fact, for a period of his ministry, Jesus taught entirely by telling stories (Mark 4:33-34). And most of them were snatched from everyday life. And of course, God used contemporary dramas to reach his people, even before Jesus was born. Read through the book of Esther and try to find a reference to God. It's not there. But in the background, God is always present. Just like in real life.

Use these sketches to bring up issues that the pastor's message will address and questions that his sermon will answer.

Telling It Like It Is

Summary: Chris has just finished an invention to help Christians witness more effectively. But when his friend Lenny shows up, things don't go quite as planned.

Purpose: To show that effective witnessing means using language people can understand.

Time: 5-7 minutes

Tone: Lighthearted

Cast: Chris — A curious and slightly goofy guy (male);
Lenny — His clever and inventive friend (male)

Props/Set: A pager, an Off-stage buzzer of some sort, electrical wires, tools, a workbench

Themes: Assumptions, communication, conversion, evangelism, listening, missions, new life, witnessing

Text: "We are therefore Christ's ambassadors, as though God were making his appeal through us. We implore you on Christ's behalf: Be reconciled to God" (2 Corinthians 5:20).

Notes: You'll need a stagehand to make the sound effects. The sketch will be more fun if Chris really jumps and jolts and jives when the device goes off. Picture someone with a chicken in his pants getting struck by lightning. That's what he should look like. The script is written with college-age actors in mind. You may need to make a few wording changes if you use older actors.

1   *SETTING:* Lenny's garage. He is tinkering with his newest invention.
2   Tools and electrical paraphernalia are scattered across the table.
3   As the scene opens, Chris enters and wants to find out what Lenny
4   is up to.
5
6   CHRIS: Hey Lenny, whatcha working on?
7   LENNY: Hi, Chris. This is my latest invention. I call it my Evango-
8   Pager Witnessing Simulation Device.
9   CHRIS: *(Peering down at it.)* Cool.
10 LENNY: It looks like a normal pager, but it's *different.*
11 CHRIS: Different? How?
12 LENNY: It's different because you can use it for witnessing to
13   people. You know, telling them about Jesus!
14 CHRIS: Wow! How does it work?
15 LENNY: Well, here, let me show you. Just clip it on your belt like
16   this. *(Clipping it onto CHRIS's belt)* There. Now I just turn it on,
17   and — presto!
18 CHRIS: Presto what? It didn't do anything.
19 LENNY: Say something to me. Anything about Jesus. Pretend I've
20   never gone to church and don't know anything about him
21   except that he's famous and lived a long time ago.
22 CHRIS: OK. Sure. No problem. *(CHRIS walks back across the stage*
23   *and approaches LENNY once again. They both take on a new*
24   *personality.)* Hey, buddy. Do you have a minute?
25 LENNY: Yeah? What do you want?
26 CHRIS: I just wanted to ask you a few questions. If you were to die
27   today, where would you go?
28 LENNY: The graveyard.
29 CHRIS: No, I mean, are you saved? *(Buzz)* Ah! What was that?
30 LENNY: That was my Evango-Pager Witnessing Simulation Device
31   at work! If I weren't a Christian, I wouldn't know what
32   you're talking about. I'd wonder, "Saved from what?"
33 CHRIS: So it buzzes every time I say something that a non-
34   Christian wouldn't understand?
35 LENNY: Yup. And gives you a little shock as a reminder not to say

1   something the Bible doesn't teach.
2   CHRIS: OK, no problem. This'll be easy. Let me try again. Sir,
3   have you ever been born again? *(Buzz)* **Converted?**
4   *(Buzz)***Have you ever accepted Jesus?** *(Buzz. Each time, CHRIS*
5   *gets more and more wildly electrocuted.)* **Ouch! Come on, now!**
6   **You said you'd heard of Jesus!**
7   LENNY: Yeah, but many people don't know what you mean by
8   "accepted" Jesus. Do you mean accept that he lived? Accept
9   that he was a real person? Accept that he was God? There's a
10   big difference between believing that he lived and personally
11   trusting in him as the one who paid the debt for all the wrongs
12   you've ever done.
13 CHRIS: All right. Let's try this one more time … Hey, dude, are
14   you happy?
15 LENNY: No, man. I lost my job at Flippo Burger, my girlfriend
16   started dating the captain of the football team, and my pet
17   turtle ran away. Why? Are you like a shrink or something?
18 CHRIS: No. I'm a Christian. And I'm here today to tell you there
19   is an answer to your problems! As soon as you acce — I mean,
20   trust in Jesus as your Savior, your troubles will be gone! You'll
21   never have to worry about money again! Girls will fall all over
22   you! You'll learn how to win friends and influence people!
23   *(Buzz!)*
24 LENNY: The Bible doesn't teach all that! Jesus never claimed he'd
25   make our lives easier, just that he'd be there to give us real
26   hope during the tough times. Listen, give it one more try.
27   Here, I'll turn it down from "non-Christian" to "occasional
28   church-goer." *(Readjusts the device.)*
29 CHRIS: *(A little hesitantly)* **OK** … If you were to die today, would
30   you go to heaven?
31 LENNY: Sure. I go to church. Who doesn't? I never smoke or do
32   drugs. I'm a pretty good person.
33 CHRIS: But pretty good isn't good enough. God demands that we
34   be perfect …
35 LENNY: *(As himself)* Keep going, you're getting the hang of it.

1 CHRIS: *(Says very fast, in one breath.)* **You see, in his divine**
2 **sovereignty, the triune God declared that his only begotten**
3 **Son offer his life as a propitiation for your sins and for eternal**
4 **reconciliation. So the promised Messiah vicariously suffered**
5 **to redeem you from eternal damnation during his crucifixion**
6 **and subsequent exaltation. But by his resurrection from the**
7 **dead, your sins have been atoned for and you** — *(Buzz! Buzz!*
8 *Buzz! CHRIS falls to ground and writhes.)*
9 LENNY: **Oh, no! You broke it!**
10 CHRIS: *(Getting up)* **That thing is dangerous! It'll never catch on.**
11 **It's too much work saying things in ways people can**
12 **understand!**
13 LENNY: **Oh? Then how did you ever become a Christian?**
14 CHRIS: **That was different.**
15 LENNY: **How?**
16 CHRIS: **Well, when I was just a kid, my grandma just told me God**
17 **loves me. She said that even though I've been bad, Jesus is**
18 **good. She said if I'd trust in Jesus, God wouldn't punish me**
19 **but would hug me forever.**
20 LENNY: **She said God would hug you forever?**
21 CHRIS: **Yeah. Would your Evango-Pager Witnessing Simulation**
22 **Device have beeped her for saying that?**
23 LENNY: **I don't think so … The whole point of witnessing is telling**
24 **people what they need to hear in words they can understand.**
25 *(Holding up the device)* **All this thing does is remind people of**
26 **that.**
27 CHRIS: **Hmmm. Maybe it's not such a bad invention after all.**
28 **Here, let me help you fix it.** *(They both lean over the device and*
29 *begin tinkering with it as the lights fade out.)*
30
31
32
33
34
35

Great Atmosphere

Summary: Tony has invited all his friends to his favorite restaurant, but he is too embarrassed to invite anyone to his church.

Purpose: To explore why people are ashamed to invite their friends to church.

Time: 3-5 minutes

Tone: Lighthearted until the end

Cast: Tony — A guy who recently discovered a great place to eat (male); Erik — His insightful friend (male)

Props/Set: Plates, napkins, silverware, and drinks; restaurant table and two chairs; if desired, have a large pizza on the table

Themes: Church issues, evangelism, excuses, missions, priorities, witnessing

Text: "If anyone is ashamed of me and my words, the Son of Man will be ashamed of him when he comes in his glory and in the glory of the Father and of the holy angels" (Luke 9:26).

Notes: Tony is a real "back-patting" kind of guy. Erik is thoughtful. If desired, you could use other actors or ambiance sounds in the background for setting the scene. Keep the dialog lively — remember that they're supposed to be having a great time.

1 **SETTING:** A popular restaurant after church. As the scene opens, Tony
2   and Erik are seated at a table together.
3
4 **TONY: So what do you think? Is this place great, or is this place**
5   **great?**
6 **ERIK: This place is great!**
7 **TOGETHER: Yeah!** *(They slap each other a high five.)*
8 **TONY: Just like I told you.**
9 **ERIK: Just like you told me! You're the man!**
10 **TONY: I'm the man!**
11 **TOGETHER: Yeah!** *(They slap another high five.)*
12 **ERIK: I gotta hand it to you. You found the best restaurant in**
13   **town. And everybody's here! I never knew so many people**
14   **went out to eat after church!**
15 **TONY: Sure, happens every week.** *(Leaning forward and whispering)*
16   **But you gotta hurry to get here before the** _____
17   *(Insert a local denomination other than your own)* **do. Those**
18   _____ *(Insert denomination)* **love their food!**
19 **ERIK: Boy, me too. And I've been missing out! The food looks**
20   **great and the atmosphere is nice. And all my friends are here!**
21 **TONY: Everyone's here! It's a great place!**
22 **ERIK: Yeah!** *(Waving to friends)* **Look, it's that guy from choir!**
23 **TONY: Jerod?**
24 **ERIK: Jeremy.** *(Waving)* **Hey, Jeremy!** *(Looking toward an imaginary*
25   *pizza)* **Look at that! Whoa, baby! Now, that's what I'm talking**
26   **about!** *(To TONY)* **Check out the size of that pizza!**
27 **TONY: Whoa. That's the mother of all pizzas!**
28 **ERIK: You could say that again!**
29 **TONY: Whoa. That's the mother of all pizzas!** *(They pause and look*
30   *at each other as if to say, "That joke was really old.")* **Just like I**
31   **told you!**
32 **ERIK: You're the man!**
33 **TONY: I'm the man!** *(Another high five)*
34 **ERIK:** *(Starting to eat the meal or drink water; this can be mimed)*
35   **Say, how did you find out about this place, anyway?**

1   TONY: *(With his mouth full of food)* **Oh, Adrian, this guy at work,**
2   **comes here all the time. He introduced me to the place a**
3   **couple months ago, and I've been coming here ever since.**
4   ERIK: **Oh, really?**
5   TONY: **And then, of course, I started inviting people from church.**
6   **And now, voila! Hey, look! It's some of the people from our**
7   **small group Bible study!** *(Calling Off-stage)* **Hey, Suzanne!**
8   **Good to see you! How's that baby?**
9   ERIK: **So is he here?**
10   TONY: **Who? Suzanne's baby?**
11   ERIK: **No, Adrian — the guy from work. Does he come here after**
12   **church, too?**
13   TONY: **Oh. I don't know. I don't think he goes to church.**
14   ERIK: **Oh.**
15   TONY: **Hey, look, there's Pastor Bob! Hey, Pastor Bob! How do**
16   **you like that pizza? Isn't this place great? Kinda like the**
17   **Garden of Eatin'! Get it, Pastor? Garden of Eatin'!** *(To*
18   *himself)* **Oh, I kill myself.** *(Chuckling)*
19   ERIK: **Did you ever invite him to church?**
20   TONY: **Erik, he's there every week! He's the pastor.**
21   ERIK: **No, I mean that Adrian guy. Did you ever invite him to go**
22   **to church with you?**
23   TONY: *(Finally focusing on the conversation)* **No ... I guess I never**
24   **even thought about it.**
25   ERIK: **Why not?**
26   TONY: **I don't know. Inviting someone to church?! I mean, that's**
27   **not really me, you know. He might think I'm some kind of**
28   **fanatic or something. It'd be a little embarrassing.**
29   ERIK: **Embarrassing? Why?**
30   TONY: **Well, you know ...** *(Trying to be funny)* **What if he wasn't too**
31   **excited about what was on the menu? Look, forget about him**
32   **and have some pizza. Relax. Enjoy yourself. I mean, look**
33   **around you! I'm telling you, everyone is here!**
34   ERIK: **Yeah, everyone ... except ... Adrian.** *(Slow fadeout)*
35

The Truth Mantra

Summary: Steve is trying to convince Gary that Truth doesn't exist. Gary gets more and more confused as he tries to follow Steve's bizarre reasoning.

Purpose: To show the foolishness and folly of relativism.

Time: 5-7 minutes

Tone: Lighthearted

Cast: Steve — An enthusiastic adherent to relativism (male); Gary — A seeker of truth confused by his friend's doubletalk (male)

Props/Set: A CD of instrumental "New Age" music, candles, boom box, couch

Themes: Guilt, hope, reality, relativism, truth

Text: "Even as he spoke, many put their faith in him. To the Jews who had believed him, Jesus said, 'If you hold to my teaching, you are really my disciples. Then you will know the truth, and the truth will set you free'" (John 8:30-32).

Notes: Many people today claim that each of us constructs his or her "personal truth." This sketch reveals how foolish this view is. As Gary says, "Nobody makes up truth ... The only thing you get to decide is how you're gonna respond to it." Keep the exchanges humorous and quick.

1   *SETTING:* Steve's living room. As the scene opens, both men are
2   seated in a lotus position. Steve has his hands on his knees, thumb
3   and forefinger closed in a circle. Gary is watching him
4   suspiciously. In the background, mellow "new age" music is
5   playing and large candles are burning.
6
7   STEVE: **Are you ready to get started?**
8   GARY: **I'm not so sure about this ...**
9   STEVE: **Trust me. It'll help. Really.**
10   GARY: *(Giving in)* **All right ... What did you say this is called**
11   **again?**
12   STEVE: **The "truth mantra." It's easy — just repeat after me ...**
13   *(Becoming solemn and chanting in a monotone with his eyes*
14   *closed)* **What's true for you is true for you ...**
15   GARY: *(Staring at STEVE, still unconvinced)* **What's true for you is**
16   **true for you ...**
17   STEVE: **What's true for me is true for me ...**
18   GARY: **What's weird for you is weird for me ...** *(STEVE opens his*
19   *eyes and looks at GARY accusingly)* **OK, OK...** *(Closing his eyes*
20   *and getting really solemn)* **What's true for me is true for me ...**
21   STEVE: **We make up truth.**
22   GARY: **We make up truth.**
23   STEVE: **And then we're free.**
24   GARY: **And then we're free.**
25   STEVE: *(Slowly opening his eyes and sighing, very relaxed)* **There.**
26   **Now, don't you feel better?**
27   GARY: **That was the most embarrassing thing I've ever done. How**
28   **is that supposed to help me?**
29   STEVE: *(Sighing)* **Listen, you've been plagued with guilt for all**
30   **these things you keep telling yourself you "shouldn't have**
31   **done" or "shouldn't have said." But you shouldn't say things**
32   **like that! You see, the whole problem is you think some things**
33   **are right and others are wrong. But that's just not right. The**
34   **one thing you need to understand is that truth doesn't exist.**
35   GARY: *(Rapid-fire conversation, in Abbott and Costello "Who's on*

1   *First?" style)* **So, what word shouldn't I say?**
2   **STEVE: Shouldn't.**
3   **GARY: And thinking that there's right and wrong, is wrong?**
4   **STEVE: Right.**
5   **GARY: And the truth is, there's no truth?**
6   **STEVE: Exactly.**
7   **GARY: There's no such thing as absolute truth?**
8   **STEVE: That's right.**
9   **GARY: Are you sure?**
10   **STEVE: Absolutely.**
11   **GARY:** *(Does a double-take at STEVE and tries to let all that settle in.)*
12   **Well, how do you know that's true?**
13   **STEVE: Huh?**
14   **GARY: How do you know the truth mantra is true?!**
15   **STEVE: Well, truth depends on what you believe. And I believe it's**
16   **true, therefore it is.**
17   **GARY: I always thought some things were true regardless of what**
18   **you believe.**
19   **STEVE: That's your problem. Once you grasp the truth of the**
20   **truth mantra, your eyes will be opened to the falsehood of**
21   **truth.**
22   **GARY:** *(Looking around suspiciously)* **Am I on** *Candid Camera* **or**
23   **something?**
24   **STEVE: No ... Listen, you just need to set aside your doubts and**
25   **trust that I'm right.**
26   **GARY: Because it's true for you?**
27   **STEVE: Right.**
28   **GARY: Well, I don't believe you're right!**
29   **STEVE: Now you're being intolerant, and I'm afraid that's just not**
30   **acceptable.**
31   **GARY: Let me get this straight: Saying that something is true is**
32   **intolerant.**
33   **STEVE: Right.**
34   **GARY: Because the only thing that's true is that nothing is true.**
35   **STEVE: Uh-huh.**

1 GARY: And the only thing that's not tolerated is intolerance.

2 STEVE: *(Very pleased)* Now you're catching on.

3 GARY: I have no idea what I just said ...

4 STEVE: Well, should we go through the truth mantra one more

5   time for tonight?

6 GARY: I guess. But I don't really think it has any truth to it ...

7 STEVE: That's OK. If you just repeat it to yourself often enough,

8   you'll start to believe it, and that's what counts! OK, here we

9   go ... *(Same solemn posture and voice)* What's true for you is

10   true for you ...

11 GARY: *(Grudgingly)* What's true for you is true for you ...

12 STEVE: What's true for me is true for me ...

13 GARY: What's true for me is — wait a minute. By trying to get me

14   to believe in your truth mantra, aren't you saying that it's

15   true for me?

16 STEVE: Of course.

17 GARY: Then you're saying that what's true for you is really true

18   for me?

19 STEVE: No way! I would never impose my truth on you!

20 GARY: Oh ... *(Letting that sink in)* So it boils down to this: I get to

21   decide what's true and what isn't?

22 STEVE: That's right.

23 GARY: OK, then I say absolute truth exists.

24 STEVE: Great. It exists for you.

25 GARY: And everything I believe is true.

26 STEVE: Good for you! Now you're getting the hang of it.

27 GARY: Therefore, I'm always right!

28 STEVE: See? Isn't this more fun than feeling guilty all the time?

29 GARY: And because of that, everyone who disagrees with me is

30   wrong!

31 STEVE: Wait a minute.

32 GARY: *(Really getting into it now)* One plus one is no longer two!

33   Gravity doesn't affect me! I have x-ray vision! I can walk

34   through walls! I will never grow old! No one else can tell me

35   what to think! *(Pointing to STEVE)* And everything you own is

1   now mine! I win! I win!
2 STEVE: You can't do that.
3 GARY: Do what?
4 STEVE: Change the laws of gravity and time and space. And take
5   my stuff.
6 GARY: Why not? My truth is that what's true for me is true for
7   everyone!
8 STEVE: Now you're confusing me.
9 GARY: Then we're even! This has been absolutely the stupidest
10   conversation I've ever had in my life! None of it makes any
11   sense at all! *(Settling down a little bit)* **Nobody makes up truth.**
12   **That's why it's called truth. The only thing you get to decide**
13   **is how you're gonna respond to it. And I've decided how I'm**
14   **gonna respond to you and your truth mantra!**
15 STEVE: How's that?
16 GARY: **I'm gonna take my CD and go home!** *(Getting up, grabbing*
17   *boom box and leaving)*
18 STEVE: **Then you'll still have all that guilt!**
19 GARY: *(Quickly, so it doesn't sound "preachy")* **Lying to yourself**
20   **about the world doesn't change the world. I'd rather feel**
21   **guilty than know I'm living a lie. See you later, Steve. I'm**
22   **outta here.**
23 STEVE: *(Going back to the truth mantra position)* **What's true for**
24   **you is true for you. What's true for me is true for me. We**
25   **make up truth. And then we're** *(As he says the last word he*
26   *opens his eyes and realizes he's not making sense)* **free?** *(Freeze.*
27   *Fadeout.)*
28
29
30
31
32
33
34
35

The Nine-to-Fivers

Summary: Vinnie and Eddie start talking about the significance of their lives and realize that neither of them has done anything all that memorable or important.

Purpose: To get people thinking about death and the real meaning of life.

Time: 4-6 minutes

Tone: Serious, with lighthearted moments

Cast: Eddie — A man who likes to read the obituaries (male); Vinnie — His friend who'd rather read the comics (male)

Props/Set: Newspaper, water cooler, table and chairs, soda and snack machines

Themes: Death, hope, life, meaning, purpose, questions, work

Text: "The thief comes only to steal and kill and destroy; I have come that they may have life, and have it to the full" (John 10:10).

Notes: Vinnie and Eddie are hard-working guys and good friends. They joke around and sometimes give each other a hard time. In this sketch, let their friendship be evident, but let the seriousness of their conversation sink in to the audience.

1   *SETTING:* A break room at a factory. As the scene opens, Eddie is
2   seated behind the table reading the newspaper. Vinnie enters and
3   approaches the snack machine.
4
5   **VINNIE: Hey, Eddie, how ya doing?**
6   **EDDIE: Hey, Vinnie. Doing good.**
7   **VINNIE:** *(Peering over EDDIE's shoulder)* **Is that what I think it is?**
8   **EDDIE: What?**
9   **VINNIE: You're reading the obituaries again, aren't you?**
10 **EDDIE:** *(Embarrassed)* **Yup.**
11 **VINNIE: Making sure you're not dead yet?**
12 **EDDIE** *(Chuckling)* **Yeah.**
13 **VINNIE: You look pretty alive to me!**
14 **EDDIE: I'm hanging in there.**
15 **VINNIE:** *(After a pause)* **Seriously, why are you always reading**
16   **through the obituaries like that?**
17 **EDDIE: It's interesting.**
18 **VINNIE: It's creepy.**
19 **EDDIE: I like to know who's still alive.**
20 **VINNIE:** *(Offhandedly)* **Or who's not.**
21 **EDDIE: Oh, man! Look at this! Fredrick Manning died of a heart**
22   **attack!**
23 **VINNIE: I never heard of the guy.**
24 **EDDIE: Me neither. It says he worked as a mechanic down there**
25   **on Ridgeland Drive. No kids. No wife. Whoa, just forty-two**
26   **years old!**
27 **VINNIE: C'mon, man, you're freaking me out!**
28 **EDDIE: Here's one about a lady who slipped in her bathtub and**
29   **drowned.**
30 **VINNIE: Eddie!**
31 **EDDIE:** *(Putting the paper down)* **A whole life summed up in one**
32   **paragraph written by some reporter you don't even know**
33   **who'd rather be covering the 4-H club's bake sale. Just one**
34   **paragraph — printed today, glanced over by a few people,**
35   **and then tossed in the trash tomorrow. That's it. That's all you**

1   get. One paragraph.

2   VINNIE: I'd rather read the comics.

3   EDDIE: Most people would.

4   VINNIE: *(Going over to the snack machine)* What's that supposed to

5   mean?

6   EDDIE: Oh, just that most people would rather laugh a little and

7   then flip the page than really consider the fact that they're an

8   obituary waiting to be written.

9   VINNIE: Eddie, my friend, you need professional help.

10   EDDIE: So my wife tells me ... So what do you think they'll put in

11   mine?

12   VINNIE: *(Getting a snack)* Huh?

13   EDDIE: You know, what's my paragraph gonna say?

14   VINNIE: Um ... I don't know.

15   EDDIE: C'mon, give it a shot! Pretend you're the reporter.

16   VINNIE: All right ... Eddie Bertolus ... He was born, he read the

17   paper a lot, he freaked out his fellow workers. *(Tossing him a*

18   *Twinkie)* He liked to eat Twinkies.

19   EDDIE: *(Unwrapping the snack)* I'm serious. What do you think

20   they'd write?

21   VINNIE: I don't know. What does it matter? You won't be around

22   to read it anyway.

23   EDDIE: You'd read it, wouldn't you?

24   VINNIE: *(Sighing)* Sure, Eddie. I promise to skip the comics that

25   day. I promise I'll read your paragraph. Even though I've

26   known you for twenty years, I'll read your paragraph.

27   EDDIE: OK, smart aleck, what do you think they'll write about

28   you?

29   VINNIE: Um ... Vinnie Rigatoni —

30   EDDIE: *(Jokingly)* Sounds like an Italian restaurant —

31   VINNIE: Hey! Hey! *(Clearing his throat)* Vinnie Rigatoni. He was

32   born, he read the comics a lot, he put up with weird

33   coworkers, *(Unwrapping a snack of his own)* and he liked

34   Twinkies, too.

35   EDDIE: Is that really how you want people to remember you?

1   **VINNIE:** Quit kidding yourself, Eddie. No one's gonna remember
2   guys like us.
3   **EDDIE:** What do you mean?
4   **VINNIE:** We're nobodies. We're not important or famous or rich.
5   We didn't invent anything or star in any movies or win any
6   wars. We're the nameless nine-to-fivers. *(Acting this out as he*
7   *tells his story)* Like those ensigns on *Star Trek* who beam down
8   to the planet —
9   **TOGETHER:** And they never beam back up!
10   **VINNIE:** Right! You know, like, "Ensign Vinnie, go check out that
11   cave over there!" "OK, Captain!" *(Peering under the table,*
12   *pretending to be attacked by an alien creature)* **Zap!** "Ah! A
13   Mugolian lizard! *(Dramatically pretending to die)* Ugh."
14   *(Standing up)* See? And then everyone else goes back to the
15   ship for a briefing about the mission and no one misses them.
16   **EDDIE:** A Mugolian lizard, huh? I think I saw that episode.
17   **VINNIE:** Well, it's always the same: They rename the aliens, they
18   rename the planets, and they just get a couple more ensigns
19   for each new show. Guys like us just haven't done anything
20   significant enough to get our names in the credits.
21   **EDDIE:** Yeah, well, my seventy-one-yard touchdown run helped us
22   beat Lancaster High in the state semifinals back in high
23   school —
24   **VINNIE:** Yeah, I remember — that was a great catch, but how is
25   that gonna change the world? I mean, think of how many
26   people live on this planet. How many are actually
27   remembered? Only a handful. And at best you get a few lines
28   in a history book that nobody wants to read anyway. The truth
29   is, no one's gonna remember guys like us. We're just not
30   important enough.
31   **EDDIE:** Thanks for the pick-me-up.
32   **VINNIE:** Well, that's life.
33   **EDDIE:** *(Pause)* Doesn't that bother you?
34   **VINNIE:** Look, I told you before, I prefer not to think about it …
35   You want a soda?

1   EDDIE: No thanks ... So you think that's it? Get born, read the
2   comics, and die?
3   VINNIE: I guess. And eat stuff that's bad for you. And work a lot.
4   And go fishing sometimes ... It doesn't make for very good
5   reading, does it?
6   EDDIE: No, it doesn't ... Don't you think there's more to life than
7   that?
8   VINNIE: I don't know ... *(A buzzing sound is heard from Off-stage)*
9   C'mon, that's us. Break's over. Time to get back to work,
10   Ensign Eddie. *(VINNIE exits.)*
11   EDDIE: *(Stands, folds the paper, and mumbles reflectively to himself.)*
12   He was born, *(Touches the paper)* he read the paper a lot,
13   *(Picks up his snack wrapper)* he liked to eat Twinkies, he caught
14   a football one time, and then *(Pause)* he died ... *(Freeze.*
15   *Fadeout.)*
16
17
18
19
20
21
22
23
24
25
26
27
28
29
30
31
32
33
34
35

The Cleaning Guys

Summary: When Joey hires Billy Bob to help him clean an office suite, things start to go wrong. But Joey's not worried. After all, his motto is, "If you can't fix it, cover it up!"

Purpose: To show how people would rather cover up problems than fix them.

Time: 3-5 minutes

Tone: Lighthearted

Cast: Joey — The owner of an office-cleaning agency (male);
Billy Bob — His klutzy coworker (male)

Props/Set: Duct tape, vacuum, a fast-food drink and cheeseburger, framed picture, vase or lamp (pre-broken and taped together from the inside), headphones, end table, janitor cart filled with cleaning supplies, two office chairs, a white rug

Themes: Coping, excuses, hiding, integrity, purity, secrets, sin, spiritual health

Text: "Then I acknowledged my sin to you and did not cover up my iniquity. I said, 'I will confess my transgressions to the Lord' — and you forgave the guilt of my sin. *Selah*" (Psalm 32:5).

Notes: This sketch is very physical, so having actors who are skilled in physical comedy would be a plus. When directing this sketch, keep in mind that the movement, timing, and nonverbal communication are key.

1   ***SETTING:*** After hours in an office suite. As the scene opens, Joey is
2   pushing a janitor's cart filled with cleaning supplies. Billy Bob is
3   pushing a vacuum cleaner with one hand and holding a
4   cheeseburger and drink in the other.
5
6   **JOEY: Take a look at this place, Billy Bob!**
7   **BILLY BOB:** *(Looking around)* **All right!**
8   **JOEY: High class, huh?!**
9   **BILLY BOB: What's this place called again, Joey?**
10   **JOEY: Premier Financial Concepts.**
11   **BILLY BOB: It's a lot nicer than that real estate office you used to**
12   **clean.** *(Takes a sip of his soda, then runs his hand along the edge*
13   *of the desk.)*
14   **JOEY: No kidding.** *(Slapping BILLY BOB's fingers)* **And there's a lot**
15   **of fragile stuff here, so be careful!**
16   **BILLY BOB: Of course I'll be careful. This is me we're talking**
17   **about!**
18   **JOEY: That's what I'm afraid of. Look, the people who own this**
19   **place are loaded with dough, which is why I landed the job**
20   **cleaning the joint. Good pay. Good hours. And not a whole lot**
21   **of work.**
22   **BILLY BOB: Hey, thanks for hiring me to work with you this**
23   **month, Joey! I mean, since I lost that job at Jumbo Burger ...**
24   *(Takes a bite of his burger.)*
25   **JOEY: Not a problem. Look, we gotta get started. I'm gonna start**
26   **with that desk over there. You start vacuuming over here by**
27   **the chair. By the way, why'd you get fired from Jumbo Burger**
28   **anyway?**
29   **BILLY BOB: Oh, I broke a few things while I was working there.**
30   **JOEY:** *(Uneasily)* **How many things?**
31   **BILLY BOB: Less than a dozen.**
32   **JOEY:** *(Walking over to get to work)* **Great.**
33   **BILLY BOB: OK, here we go!** *(JOEY goes to the other part of the*
34   *stage. As BILLY BOB is cleaning, he sets down his cup of soda*
35   *and a moment later, accidentally knocks it over. The drink spills*

1   *on the rug. He tries splashing it back in the cup, sucking it up with*
2   *a straw, soaking it up with his shirt, and scrubbing at it, but he*
3   *can't get the stain out.)* **Um ... Hey, Joey?**
4   **JOEY:** *(Still cleaning)* **Yeah.**
5   **BILLY BOB: There's a stain in the carpet over here.**
6   **JOEY: So scrub it out.**
7   **BILLY BOB: I tried.**
8   **JOEY:** *(Coming over to check it out)* **Hmmm. Looks fresh.** *(Dipping*
9   *his finger in it and licking his finger)* **Wait a minute. This tastes**
10   **like Cherry Coke! Did you spill your drink?**
11   **BILLY BOB: Uh —**
12   **JOEY: Billy Bob!**
13   **BILLY BOB:** *(Trying to change the subject)* **Want a bite of my**
14   **burger?**
15   **JOEY: Billy Bob, listen to me! We're supposed to be cleaning up —**
16   **not making more of a mess!**
17   **BILLY BOB: Yeah, I know.**
18   **JOEY: Oh, well. It's no big deal. You know our motto ...**
19   **BILLY BOB: Right ... Um, which motto is that?**
20   **JOEY: "If you can't fix it, cover it up!"**
21   **BILLY BOB: If you can't fix it, cover it up! I like that motto.**
22   **JOEY: Right! Just pull that end table over to this side of the couch,**
23   **and no one will ever notice. And be careful!**
24   **BILLY BOB: Great!** *(As he works)* **If you can't fix it, cover it up ...**
25   *(JOEY puts on his headphones and goes back to work on the other*
26   *part of the stage. BILLY BOB pulls the end table over, but in the*
27   *process, a lamp or vase tips off, hits the floor, and shatters. JOEY*
28   *is wearing headphones and doesn't notice. BILLY BOB gathers all*
29   *the pieces together and pulls out a roll of duct tape. He tapes the*
30   *vase together and puts it back on the end table.)* **If you can't fix**
31   **it, cover it up!**
32   **JOEY:** *(Taking off headphones)* **How's it going over there?**
33   **BILLY BOB:** *(Stepping in front of the vase so JOEY can't see it)* **Good,**
34   **Joey!**
35   **JOEY: Great. There's one last thing we need to do. See that**

1   **painting on the wall over there? They want it dusted. You**
2   **wanna tackle that and I'll finish the vacuuming?**
3   **BILLY BOB:** *(Looking at it carefully)* **Is that an expensive painting?**
4   **JOEY: Very.**
5   **BILLY BOB:** *(Taking a deep breath)* **OK.** *(JOEY puts on his*
6   *headphones and starts vacuuming. As he vacuums, it becomes*
7   *evident that he is dancing to the music, becoming a little oblivious*
8   *to what's going on behind him where BILLY BOB is sizing up the*
9   *picture. BILLY BOB reaches up to dust it, but finds that it is a*
10   *little too high. So he pulls the end table over, stacks the chair on*
11   *top of it, and tries to dust the very top of the painting. Meanwhile,*
12   *JOEY is backing up and knocks into the stack just as BILLY BOB*
13   *grabs the painting and he topples to the floor, pulling the painting*
14   *down over his head. They stare at each other for a moment, then*
15   *at the mess, then back at each other.)*
16   **TOGETHER: If you can't fix it, cover it up!** *(BILLY BOB pulls out*
17   *the duct tape, yanks out an arm's length of it, and they freeze.*
18   *Blackout.)*

Just the Two of Us

Summary: Meredith is all set for a romantic weekend getaway alone with her husband, but it doesn't look like they're going to be alone after all!

Purpose: To show how easily we get distracted from pursuing intimacy in marriage.

Time: 4-6 minutes

Tone: Lighthearted

Cast: Glen — A busy businessman who's been neglecting his wife (male); Meredith — His frustrated wife (female)

Props/Set: Cell phone, pager, briefcase, laptop computer, palmtop computer, popular novel, file folders, magazines, recharge cords and batteries, dictation tape recorder, CD player and CDs, briefcase, purse, table

Themes: Addictions, ambition, distractions, love, married life, modern life, priorities, relationships, rest, stress, work

Text: "Then, because so many people were coming and going that they did not even have a chance to eat, he said to them, 'Come with me by yourselves to a quiet place and get some rest'" (Mark 6:31).

Notes: Meredith is frustrated but not belligerent, so keep the tone of the sketch lighthearted.

1   *SETTING:* The living room of their house. Meredith and Glen are
2   packed and ready for a romantic weekend getaway. Glen is On-
3   stage, closing up his briefcase.
4
5   **MEREDITH:** *(Entering, joyfully)* **Oh! I'm so excited! It's been so**
6   **long since we've gotten away together, just the two of us. I've**
7   **been looking forward to this weekend all year. So ... Dear?**
8   **Are you all packed?**
9   **GLEN: I sure am! I've got** *(As he lists these, he points to them each*
10   *in turn, delivering these lines very quickly)* **my pager, my cell**
11   **phone, my laptop, my palmtop, my portable CD player —**
12   **and a couple of my favorite CDs — tape recorder to dictate**
13   **notes, and my briefcase!**
14   **MEREDITH:** *(Shocked)* **What's in the briefcase?**
15   **GLEN:** *(Opening the briefcase and pulling out items)* **Well, let's see.**
16   **I've got the cords to recharge the cell phone, extra batteries**
17   **for the palmtop, a phone line for the computer so I can check**
18   **my e-mail, a few proposals to work on, a couple newsletters**
19   **I've been hoping to read, and the latest John Grisham thriller**
20   *(Or another popular fiction title).*
21   **MEREDITH: But I thought this was supposed to be a romantic**
22   **weekend away from work.**
23   **GLEN:** *(Kind of shocked)* **Well, it is. That's why I'm leaving the fax**
24   **machine, the cappuccino maker, and my personal secretary,**
25   **Miss Butterfield, back here!**
26   **MEREDITH: But Glen! I wanna spend the time with** *you ... all* **of**
27   **you. I don't wanna share you with John Grisham, your**
28   **clients, and your cell phone!**
29   **GLEN: But the reason I got the cell phone was for the freedom to**
30   **get away for weekends like this.**
31   **MEREDITH: But you're not getting away! You're taking it all with**
32   **you!**
33   **GLEN: That's not true.**
34   **MEREDITH: Oh, yeah? Then name one thing you use every day**
35   **at your office that you're not taking along.**

1 GLEN: *(Thoughtfully)* **The copy machine! You're right! I probably**
2 **could fit that in the back of the minivan if I took the other seat**
3 **out of the back. I knew I forgot something …**
4 **MEREDITH: Glen, I can't believe you said that!**
5 GLEN: **Yeah … I guess it would be hard to get in and out of the**
6 **elevator …**
7 **MEREDITH:** *(Sighing)* **Honey, you've been spending so much time**
8 **at work, I never see you anymore. I feel like I hardly know**
9 **you!**
10 GLEN: **C'mon now. That's not true, Elaine.**
11 **MEREDITH: Elaine? It's Meredith. Your wife, Meredith!**
12 GLEN: **Oh yeah, of course!** *(Pulling out the palmtop and saying the*
13 *letters aloud as he enters the name in)* **M-E-R-E-D-I-T-H,**
14 **relationship — wife.**
15 **MEREDITH:** *(She feigns getting angry.)* **Glen!**
16 GLEN: **I was kidding! I was only kidding.**
17 **MEREDITH: Well, I'm not kidding. I've had it. Do you want to**
18 **spend this weekend at a romantic bed and breakfast with your**
19 **wife or your work?**
20 GLEN: **Hmmm …**
21 **MEREDITH:** *(She can't believe he has to think about it.)* **Uh, Glen?!**
22 GLEN: **OK, maybe you're right … I can leave the laptop here.**
23 **MEREDITH: And the cell phone.**
24 GLEN: **Not the cell phone!**
25 **MEREDITH: It's either me or call waiting.**
26 GLEN: **OK, you win. I'll leave the cell phone, too.**
27 **MEREDITH:** *(She takes these things off his belt and lays them on the*
28 *table.)* **And the pager. And the palmtop. And the recorder. And**
29 **the CDs … And the briefcase.**
30 GLEN: **Can't I at least bring along John Grisham?**
31 **MEREDITH: No.**
32 GLEN: **But what am I gonna do all weekend?**
33 **MEREDITH:** *(Getting close and romantic)* **Spend time with *me*.**
34 *(Taking his hand)* **Hold my hand again. Walk with me along the**
35 **beach. Laugh with me like you used to.** *(Leaning close,*

1 *speaking suggestively)* **Snuggle with me.** *(Leaning closer)* **Kiss**
2 **me.**
3 **GLEN:** *(He looks into her eyes.)* **Good-bye, e-mail! Good-bye,**
4 **Internet! Good-bye, world!**
5 **MEREDITH:** *(Pulling him close)* **Hello, handsome.**
6 **GLEN: Hello … Meredith.** *(As they lean to kiss, the cell phone rings.*
7 *They both look toward it, then look back at each other.)* **Just a**
8 **minute.** *(He reaches around her, grabs the cell phone, pauses for*
9 *a moment as it continues to ring, looks at MEREDITH, then turns*
10 *it off and sets it down. They exit arm in arm. Fadeout.)*
11
12
13
14
15
16
17
18
19
20
21
22
23
24
25
26
27
28
29
30
31
32
33
34
35

The Conference

Summary: Mrs. Carver has started assuming too much about the parents of the children in her fifth-grade class. When George Hopland comes into her room, she is in for a big surprise.

Purpose: To show how prejudice and assumptions can get you into trouble.

Time: 4-6 minutes

Tone: Lighthearted

Cast: Mrs. Carver — A flustered and stressed-out teacher (female); George Hopland — The janitor who walks into her room unawares (male)

Props/Set: Pack of bubble gum, baseball cap, papers and grade books, an overstuffed file, teacher's desk with paraphernalia, wastebasket filled with papers

Themes: Assumptions, family life, judging, parenting, rest, role models, stereotypes, stress

Text: "If you show special attention to the man wearing fine clothes and say, 'Here's a good seat for you,' but say to the poor man, 'You stand there' or 'Sit on the floor by my feet,' have you not discriminated among yourselves and become judges with evil thoughts?" (James 2:3-4).

Notes: Have fun with this sketch. As you practice, improvise to see what other things George and Randy might have in common. If your actors are comfortable with it, add your ideas to the sketch.

1   *SETTING:* A fifth-grade classroom after school. As the scene opens,
2   Mrs. Carver is seated at a desk with a pile of notes, papers, and
3   other paraphernalia from a fifth-grade teacher's desk. A trash can
4   filled with papers sits in the corner.
5
6   MRS. CARVER: *(Complaining to herself)* **What a day! Teaching**
7   **would be a breeze if we didn't have all these parent**
8   **conferences all the time. Boy, you can really tell which of these**
9   **kids come from broken homes — and which parents actually**
10   **care about their kids. Like mother, like daughter. Like father,**
11   **like son. Let's see ... only one left.** *(Looking at her schedule)*
12   **Oh, great. This'll be a fun one. Randy's dad.** *(Sarcastically)*
13   *Randy. Randy. Randy. Randy's daddy* **... I can't wait to meet**
14   **him! If he's anything like his son ...**
15 GEORGE: *(Mimes entering a door. He looks around, noisily chewing*
16   *a large slab of gum and wearing a baseball cap.)* **Hello?**
17   **Anybody in here?**
18 MRS. CARVER: **Yes, I'm right over here. Please come in. I'm Mrs.**
19   **Carver, Randy's teacher. And you must be ...**
20 GEORGE: **Hopland, George Hopland. Pleasure to meet you,**
21   **ma'am ...**
22 MRS. CARVER: *(Under her breath, making a note on her schedule)*
23   **Hmmm ... Hopland, huh? Randy must have taken his**
24   **mother's last name ...** *(To GEORGE)* **Well, please take a seat,**
25   **Mr. Hopland.**
26 GEORGE: *(Picking up the chair)* **Where should I take it? Ha, ha,**
27   **ha.** *(She doesn't laugh.)* **Ha, ha, ha, ha, ha, ha, ha, ha, ha! Right**
28   **... Just a little joke there ... So ... OK.**
29 MRS. CARVER: **Please sit down.**
30 GEORGE: *(Shrugging his shoulders)* **All right.**
31 MRS. CARVER: **Yes ... let me start by saying, first of all, I've**
32   **enjoyed having Randy in class this year. He is a very, um ...**
33   **energetic young man. And quite ... strong-willed. That'll**
34   **serve him well —**
35 GEORGE: **Well, that's good.**

1   MRS. CARVER: Yes, well. We have been experiencing a *few*
2   problems —
3   GEORGE: Problems? *(Leaning forward)* What kind of problems?
4   MRS. CARVER: Well, let's see. *(Searching)* Where is his file? Ah!
5   There it is! *(She pulls out a huge overstuffed file folder bursting*
6   *at the seams and plops it noisily on the desk.)*
7   GEORGE: That's his file?! *(Chewing gum loudly)*
8   MRS. CARVER: From the last three weeks, yes. *(Opening the file*
9   *and reading from it)* OK, let's see. The first thing is that Randy
10   has been chewing gum in class. That's really not acceptable. It
11   can distract the other students from the lesson. *(As she says*
12   *this, GEORGE blows a huge bubble and lets it pop.)*
13   GEORGE: *(Still chewing)* Is that so?
14   MRS. CARVER: Yes. *(As she continues, GEORGE notices that his*
15   *shoe is untied. He leans over to tie it.)* He seems to be easily
16   distracted and sometimes has a difficult time staying on task
17   and focusing on one thing at a time. *(GEORGE sighs heavily*
18   *and slouches way down in his chair. MRS. CARVER continues*
19   *reading, without looking up)* Let's see ... he won't sit up
20   straight but rather slouches in his chair. *(GEORGE begins to*
21   *whistle.)* And he doesn't seem to be paying attention when I'm
22   explaining things ... *(GEORGE begins brushing lint off his*
23   *coat.)* Mr. Hopland?
24   GEORGE: Yeah?
25   MRS. CARVER: Are you listening to me?
26   GEORGE: Of course.
27   MRS. CARVER: Well, then, what have I been talking about?
28   GEORGE: *(Unsure)* Randy?
29   MRS. CARVER: *(Sighing)* He has even been belching in class.
30   GEORGE: You mean like this? *(He belches.)*
31   MRS. CARVER: Mr. Hopland!
32   GEORGE: Just checking. *(Rising as if to leave)* Is that all?
33   MRS. CARVER: Well, he always asks me to repeat everything.
34   GEORGE: Huh? What did you say?
35   MRS. CARVER: Repeat things. He always wants me to repeat

1   everything. And then, after I've repeated it, he asks me to
2   explain it to him!
3   GEORGE: What do you mean by that?
4   MRS. CARVER: I mean ... *(Exasperated)* Are you being serious?
5   GEORGE: Of course.
6   MRS. CARVER: And he openly disagrees with me!
7   GEORGE: Now, hold on there. I doubt the kid does that!
8   MRS. CARVER: He argues with me!
9   GEORGE: No, he doesn't.
10 MRS. CARVER: Yes, he does!
11 GEORGE: Does not!
12 MRS. CARVER: Does too!
13 GEORGE: Does not!
14 MRS. CARVER: *(Yelling)* Does too!
15 GEORGE: Does not!
16 MRS. CARVER: *(Starting to lose it)* I can't believe this! You're
17   acting like an immature child!
18 GEORGE: I know you are, but what am I?
19 MRS. CARVER: You're an idiot!
20 GEORGE: I know you are, but what am I?
21 MRS. CARVER: And there you stand before me, a grown man!
22 GEORGE: I know you are, but what am I?
23 MRS. CARVER: *(Gasp!)* You act just like your son!
24 GEORGE: Son? What are you talking about, lady?
25 MRS. CARVER: Your son, Randy!
26 GEORGE: I don't have a son named Randy. I'm the new
27   custodian! I just came in here to empty the garbage can.
28 MRS. CARVER: *(Shocked)* You're the janitor?
29 GEORGE: Yeah. *(Looking around)* Oh, there it is. *(Goes over, grabs*
30   *the garbage can and walks past MRS. CARVER. She is still in*
31   *shock.)* Listen, lady, you gotta be careful what you assume
32   about people. And take some time off. Go for a walk. Count to
33   ten or something. You gotta learn to relax.
34 MRS. CARVER: Relax?
35 GEORGE: *(Taking out a piece of bubble gum)* Here. Try this. Trust

1   **me. It'll help.** *(He pops some in his own mouth, starts chewing*
2   *noisily and exits. She stares down at the gum, looks up at the*
3   *audience and freezes. Blackout.)*
4
5
6
7
8
9
10
11
12
13
14
15
16
17
18
19
20
21
22
23
24
25
26
27
28
29
30
31
32
33
34
35

A Little More Deodorant

Summary: Roger just wants to finish filming his deodorant commercial, but Pamela keeps asking questions about the product.

Purpose: To show that most people would rather cover up their imperfections than admit to them.

Time: 3-5 minutes

Tone: Lighthearted

Cast: Pamela — Ditzy, naive, yet curious model (female); Roger — Big-shot director under a deadline (male)

Props/Set: Director's "first take" clicker-thing, stick of roll-on deodorant

Themes: Authenticity, hiding, modern life, purity, sin, truth

Text: "In the same way, on the outside you appear to people as righteous but on the inside you are full of hypocrisy and wickedness" (Matthew 23:28).

Notes: Use this sketch within the context of a message on being real, dealing with sin, or covering up the parts of our lives we don't want anyone else to see. The irony of this sketch is that Pamela, the naive airhead, offers insight into our own lives.

1   ***SETTING:*** The set of a TV commercial. The scene begins as Pamela
2   enters the empty stage carrying the deodorant. Roger is seated in
3   the first row of the audience. No one in the audience knows he is
4   part of the sketch.
5
6   **PAMELA:** *(Talking like an "airhead" commercial actor, but not really*
7   *into her part)* **Oh, Blitzer-Spritz's deodorant is the grandest in**
8   **the land! It can be applied without delay while using either**
9   **hand!** *(Demonstrates.)* **So do not fret or frown or fear when**
10   **odors come to call — just roll on Blitzer-Spritz's, and you can**
11   **get rid of them all!** *(Fake smile)*
12   **ROGER:** *(Leaping up from the audience)* **Cut! Cut! Cut! What is**
13   **wrong with you people? That was terrible, Pamela!**
14   **PAMELA:** *(Fluffing her hair)* **I don't think this part is worthy of my**
15   **talents.**
16   **ROGER: I don't think your talents are worthy of this part.**
17   **PAMELA: Well, I don't think —**
18   **ROGER: I know. That's the problem. Look, this is a deodorant**
19   **commercial, OK? Let's see some excitement! Some passion!**
20   **Some life! You want people to smell nice. To be confident. To**
21   **feel good about themselves! I mean, what other motivation do**
22   **you need?! You're about as excited as a dead houseplant!**
23   **PAMELA: I like flowers. Aren't flowers related to houseplants? By**
24   **the way, is my hair OK?**
25   **ROGER: Your hair is perfect. Your smile is perfect. Your face is**
26   **perfect. You even have attractive underarms. Everything is**
27   **perfect except your acting!**
28   **PAMELA: I think it stinks.**
29   **ROGER: So do I.**
30   **PAMELA: Not my acting, I mean the deodorant. I think Blitzer-**
31   **Spritz's stinks.** *(To herself)* **Hey, that's hard to say.** *(Trying to*
32   *say it five times really fast, like a tongue twister)* **I think Blitzer-**
33   **Spritz's stinks. I think Blitzer-Spritz's stinks. I think Blitzer-**
34   **Spritz's stinks. I think Blitzer-Spritz's stinks. I think Blitzer-**
35   **Spritz's stinks …**

1   **ROGER:** Pamela! This is television. It doesn't matter what you
2   think. It doesn't matter if it stinks. You're just hired to sell it,
3   not smell it.
4   **PAMELA:** *(Shocked)* But isn't that dishonest? I mean, selling
5   something I don't use! Something I don't even like! Isn't that
6   lying?
7   **ROGER:** Of course not! It's not lying, it's called ... advertising.
8   **PAMELA:** Oh.
9   **ROGER:** Look, I've got an idea ... *(To Off-stage)* Help on the set!
10   Let's get some perfume over here for Pamela. *(To PAMELA)*
11   What do you want it to smell like? Roses? Lavender? Vanilla?
12   **PAMELA:** You're just gonna cover up the smell?
13   **ROGER:** Sure, why not?
14   **PAMELA:** Can you do that? I mean, just cover up one smell with
15   another?
16   **ROGER:** This is ridiculous. Earth to Pamela! Covering things up
17   is what life is all about!
18   **PAMELA:** It is?
19   **ROGER:** Yes! Cover up the smell so no one notices, tuck in your
20   gut, get the wart removed, put on more lipstick, smear on the
21   makeup, apply some hair spray. Everybody's in the business
22   of covering up their flaws. All we're doing is making it easier
23   for them.
24   **PAMELA:** Really? How?
25   **ROGER:** We show them how messed up they are as long as they
26   don't use our product!
27   **PAMELA:** I see.
28   **ROGER:** And then we help them hide! I mean, look at you! You're
29   just an illusion. The real you is hidden so far under your
30   makeup that even Indiana Jones couldn't uncover it.
31   **PAMELA:** Really? I had no idea I was such a deep person.
32   **ROGER:** *(To himself)* Why do I put up with this?
33   **PAMELA:** But wouldn't it be better to just be real?
34   **ROGER:** Pamela, dear, it's like a game. If we all pretend, if we all
35   wear enough makeup, have enough plastic surgery, we can

1   look young forever. That way, none of us has to think about
2   what we're really like because beneath it all, everyone is
3   pretty much the same. We all stink. Which brings us back to
4   the deodorant!
5   PAMELA: To cover up the smell?
6   ROGER: Right. And no deodorant is going to fix or solve the
7   problem, no matter how nice it smells. So, Blitzer-Spritz's is as
8   good as it gets. Are you ready to try this one more time?
9   PAMELA: I think so ... What's my motivation again?
10 ROGER: *(With hands raised to the sky)* Why didn't I become a
11 dentist like my mother wanted? *(To PAMELA)* Pretend you like
12 to smell this deodorant. OK? *(Stepping Off-stage)* From the
13 top! Paste that smile on your face, and three, two, one ...
14 Action!
15 PAMELA: *(Acting as if she really likes the stuff)* Oh, Blitzer-Spritz's
16 deodorant is the grandest in the land! It can be applied
17 without delay while using either hand! *(Demonstrates.)* So do
18 not fret or frown or fear when odors come to call — just roll
19 on Blitzer-Spritz's and you can get rid of them all!
20 ROGER: *(Leaping back On-stage)* Cut! That's it! That's it! Pamela,
21 you were perfect!
22 PAMELA: *(Tossing the deodorant away)* Yuck. *(To ROGER)* But I
23 was just pretending!
24 ROGER: No one could tell, Pamela! And that's what counts. That's
25 a wrap! *(Freeze. Blackout.)*
26
27
28
29
30
31
32
33
34
35

All Shook Up

Summary: Norm is trying to check in for his flight, but everything seems to go wrong. He tries everything he can think of to deal with his anger, but in the end he loses control.

Purpose: To reveal how important it is to manage our anger.

Time: 7-9 minutes

Tone: Lighthearted

Cast: Norm — A harried businessman about to miss his flight (male); Brianna — A smart-alecky airline worker (female)

Props/Set: Cell phone, nail polish, two large overstuffed suitcases, airline ticket, one computer case, five copies of the same hardcover book, telephone, can of soda, countertop, computer keyboard and monitor, "Next Window Please" sign.

Themes: Ambition, anger, coping, frustration, modern life, patience, self-control, stress, work

Text: "A fool gives full vent to his anger, but a wise man keeps himself under control" (Proverbs 29:11).

Notes: Norm tries a variety of tricks to control his anger, but nothing works. As he gets more and more frustrated, he unconsciously shakes his can of soda. He wants to get to Denver as soon as possible, but all the airline worker wants to do is talk on the phone and do her nails. Be careful so Norm's anger doesn't build too quickly. It needs to climax at the end.

1   ***SETTING:*** The ticketing counter at an airport terminal. As the scene
2   opens, Brianna is On-stage talking on the phone behind the ticket
3   counter. Norm enters hurriedly, dragging his suitcases.
4
5   **NORM:** *(Talking on his cell phone)* **Yeah. Yeah. My flight leaves here**
6   **in a few minutes. OK. I should arrive at about seven o'clock.**
7   **Right. OK, I'm looking forward to it, too. See you soon. 'Bye.**
8   **BRIANNA:** *(Talking on a telephone, doing her nails, ignoring NORM.*
9   *There is a "Next Window Please" sign on her desk.)* **Yeah! And I**
10   **was so excited. I mean, it was Lance Williams!**
11   **NORM:** **Excuse me —**
12   **BRIANNA:** *(Ignoring him, speaking into the phone)* **Anyway, he**
13   **walked right over to me and said, "So, are you married?"**
14   **NORM:** **Excuse me!**
15   **BRIANNA:** *(She gives him a dirty look and points to the "Next*
16   *Window Please" sign. She keeps talking to her friend.)* **Can you**
17   **believe it? I couldn't believe it! I mean *the* Lance Williams**
18   **talking to me! —**
19   **NORM:** **I need to check in for this flight!**
20   **BRIANNA:** *(To NORM)* **I'm on my break.** *(To phone)* **No, I'm still**
21   **here. Yeah …**
22   **NORM:** *(Looking around)* **But you're the only one working here.**
23   **BRIANNA:** *(To phone)* **Just a minute, Lynn.** *(To NORM)* **I told you**
24   **I'm on my break. I'll be off my break at four-fifteen.** *(To the*
25   *phone)* **Anyway — so then I didn't know what to say, so —**
26   **NORM:** *(Checking his watch)* **It *is* four-fifteen!**
27   **BRIANNA:** *(Looking at her watch and counting down)* **Three-two-**
28   **one. OK. Now it's four-fifteen.** *(To the phone)* **I'll talk to you**
29   **later, Lynn. OK. 'Bye.** *(Pasting on a bright cheesy smile)* **Now,**
30   **how may I help you, sir?**
31   **NORM:** *(Handing her his ticket)* **I'm on the four-thirty flight to**
32   **Denver. I need to get my seat assignment.**
33   **BRIANNA:** **I'm sorry, that flight has already boarded.**
34   **NORM:** **What?!**
35   **BRIANNA:** **I'm sorry, sir. You need to check in twenty minutes**

1   before the flight time and be on board at least ten minutes
2   before the scheduled departure.
3   NORM: You were taking your break!
4   BRIANNA: Don't blame me, sir. You're the one who needs to
5   arrive on time.
6   NORM: *(Smiling and talking between his teeth)* Are you telling me I
7   missed my flight because you were on the phone?!
8   BRIANNA: Yes and no. Yes, you missed your flight. And no, not
9   because I was on the phone, because you didn't arrive at the
10   airport early enough.
11   NORM: *(Counting to ten under his breath, getting calmer as he does)*
12   Count to ten ... count to ten ... one-two-three-four-five-six-
13   seven-eight-nine-ten ... *(Yelling)* You can't be serious!
14   BRIANNA: *(Cheerily, tapping her watch)* Gotta be on time.
15   NORM: *(Unconsciously begins shaking his soda as he talks to her,*
16   *trying to remain in control.)* You don't understand. I've just
17   spent the last thirty minutes in a traffic jam. I'm tired. It's
18   been a long week, and —
19   BRIANNA: *(Looking down and starting to do her nails again)* You
20   missed your flight. It's probably taxiing down the runway
21   right now.
22   NORM: *(Breathing deeply, talking to himself)* In with the good ...
23   Out with the bad ... In with the good ... Out with the bad. I
24   am not getting angry. I am not getting angry. I'm in control.
25   I'm in control ...
26   BRIANNA: You should have left home earlier.
27   NORM: *(Looking up at an imaginary display board, shaking the soda*
28   *again)* What about the six-fifteen flight?
29   BRIANNA: *(Looking at her computer display)* Delayed arrival.
30   NORM: Seven forty-five?
31   BRIANNA: Already overbooked. I could put you on standby, but
32   you probably won't make it. The next earliest flight I can get
33   you confirmed on is *(Typing at a computer)* eight-o-five.
34   NORM: *(Quickly, thinking aloud)* Well, eight-o-five ... Let's see —
35   with the time change ... I guess that's not too bad. I can just

1   barely make it. Book me on that one.

2 BRIANNA: ... a.m.

3 NORM: What?!

4 BRIANNA: *(Cheerily)* Eight-o-five a.m. It's our first departure,

5   bright and early tomorrow morning. I'm sure you'll enjoy the

6   flight. We're serving a complimentary donut. You'll arrive in

7   Denver at eleven forty-five a.m.

8 NORM: I could drive to Denver faster than that!

9 BRIANNA: *(Offhandedly)* All right then. *(Handing him back his*

10   *ticket)* But that ticket is nonrefundable. We keep the four

11   hundred and ninety dollars.

12 NORM: *(With teeth clenched)* I can't fly out tomorrow morning, I

13   need to get to Denver tonight.

14 BRIANNA: *(Imitating him)* You'll have to fly out tomorrow

15   morning. You're not getting to Denver tonight. (NORM *starts*

16   *to really lose control, he shakes the cola vigorously and then*

17   *stands on one leg and begins chanting oriental, tai chi-sounding*

18   *words.)* Sir, what are you doing?

19 NORM: This is called the Resting Stork. It aligns my chakras and

20   helps me to remain in control of my inner self ... oooommmm ...

21   oooommmm ... oooommmm ... Now. I'm fine. There. I'm all

22   better.

23 BRIANNA: *(Leery)* Do you want me to put you on the eight-o-five

24   flight or just call a psychiatrist?

25 NORM: *(Speaking very slowly and distinctly, overly calm)* You need

26   to understand something. Tomorrow is too late for me to

27   arrive in Denver. I need to get to Denver before tomorrow.

28   That's why I bought an airplane ticket for tonight. Certainly

29   you can reroute me or something. Look at that ticket there.

30   *(Tapping the computer)* Check your little computer for a way to

31   get me to Denver tonight ... Go on. Tap those keys and find me

32   a way to Denver ...

33 BRIANNA: *(Sighing, picking up his ticket, and typing on her*

34   *computer)* Let's see, I could route you through Cincinnati and

35   then to Denver ... You'd arrive in Denver at four-ten a.m.

1   **NORM:** *(Shaking soda vigorously)* **This is not happening to me! Do**
2   **you know who I am?**
3   **BRIANNA:** *(Looking at his ticket)* **Norm Wright.**
4   **NORM: That's right. I am Norm Wright!**
5   **BRIANNA: How nice. I'm Brianna Forester.**
6   **NORM:** *The* **Norm Wright.**
7   **BRIANNA:** *The* **Brianna Forester.**
8   **NORM: Don't you get it?! I am** *the* **Norm Wright!**
9   **BRIANNA:** *(Smart-alecky)* **Would** *the* **Norm Wright like the four-**
10   **ten flight?**
11   **NORM: Ah!** *(Pulling at his hair and then doing a wild, out of control,*
12   *arm-flailing jig)* **What about another airline? Can they get me**
13   **there?**
14   **BRIANNA: Hmmm ... Let me see ... Why, yes ... It looks like I**
15   **could send you on United's express flight to Denver. There's**
16   **one seat left.**
17   **NORM:** *(Shocked)* **You could?**
18   **BRIANNA: Yes. You'll be in Denver at eight-thirty p.m.**
19   **NORM: Tonight?**
20   **BRIANNA: Yes.**
21   **NORM: Really?**
22   **BRIANNA: Uh-huh.**
23   **NORM: Ah. There. You see? That wasn't so bad. Now. OK. Well.**
24   **All right then.**
25   **BRIANNA: Will you be checking any bags today?**
26   **NORM: No. I'll carry these on.**
27   **BRIANNA:** *(Peering over the counter at his suitcases)* **I don't think**
28   **those bags will fit in the overhead bin.**
29   **NORM: I'll make 'em fit. Just book the flight.**
30   **BRIANNA:** *(Reaching over for them)* **I'm going to need to check**
31   **those bags.**
32   **NORM:** *(They play tug of war with one of the bags.)* **No you aren't!**
33   **BRIANNA: Yes I am!**
34   **NORM:** *(As they struggle for the bags)* **No! They're mine! Mine!**
35   **Mine! Mine!**

1   **BRIANNA: I need to check these bags!** *(Finally lets go. NORM*
2   *stumbles backward and falls down on the small bag.)* **All right.**
3   **But you have three bags. You're limited to two carry-on bags.**
4   **NORM: This one's not really a bag ... it's my computer.**
5   **BRIANNA:** *(Seeing that he is sitting on it)* ***Was* your computer ...**
6   **OK. Have those bags been with you the entire time since you**
7   **packed them?**
8   **NORM: Yes, yes, yes!**
9   **BRIANNA:** *(Handing him his boarding pass)* **Here. Don't forget**
10   **your ticket. You need to keep that with you at all times ...**
11   **Now, has anyone unknown to you asked you to carry anything**
12   **onto this flight?**
13   **NORM:** *(Very quick exchange)* **Do you mean, did they ask me**
14   **without my knowing it?**
15   **BRIANNA: No, were they unknown to you?**
16   **NORM: How could I know if they're unknown?**
17   **BRIANNA: Did anyone ask you to carry anything on this flight?!**
18   **NORM: Yes.**
19   **BRIANNA: Who?**
20   **NORM: You.**
21   **BRIANNA: Me?**
22   **NORM: Yes!**
23   **BRIANNA: When?**
24   **NORM: Just now!**
25   **BRIANNA: What are you talking about?**
26   **NORM:** *(Starting to lose control again, waving the ticket above his*
27   *head)* **You just told me to carry this ticket with me at all times!**
28   **BRIANNA: No, sir, I'm sorry, that's your old ticket.** *(Looking down*
29   *for his new ticket, noticing the computer)* **Here ... whoop.**
30   **NORM: What whoop? What? What does whoop mean?**
31   **BRIANNA: Whoop means *the* Norm Wright just missed another**
32   **flight because he wouldn't check his bags like a good**
33   **passenger.** *(Pointing to the screen)* **See? While you were**
34   **arguing with me, United express booked that last seat. They**
35   **do have precedence, you know. I'm sorry. We're back to four-**

1   **ten a.m. or tomorrow morning with the donut.**
2   **NORM:** *Ahhh! (He shakes the soda vigorously, then opens it. It sprays*
3   *him in the face, and he totally loses control. He throws the bags*
4   *down, jumps up and down on them, and screams.)* **I need to get to**
5   **Denver tonight! I am the keynote speaker at a national**
6   **conference!**
7   **BRIANNA:** **Really? What were you supposed to speak on?**
8   **NORM: My new book!**
9   **BRIANNA: What's it called?**
10   **NORM:** *Anger Management in the Real World. (Kneeling down,*
11   *reaching into his suitcase, screaming now)* **I am an expert on**
12   **anger management! Here.** *(Rummaging through his stuff,*
13   *tossing clothes all over the stage and throwing the books at her)*
14   **Have a copy! Have another one! Here's one for your little**
15   **friend on the phone! Here, send the pilot one. How about that**
16   **guy who got my seat? Why not?!**
17   **BRIANNA:** *(Looking at her watch)* **Whoop. Well, looky what time**
18   **it is.**
19   **NORM: What whoop? What? Why another whoop?**
20   **BRIANNA: Time for my next break!** *(Grabs the phone, puts up the*
21   *"Next Window Please" sign. NORM leans back and faints.*
22   *BRIANNA does her nails again and talks into the phone.)* **Yeah,**
23   **Lynn? You're never gonna believe this. I just met Norm**
24   **Wright! Yeah, *the* Norm Wright …** *(Freeze. Blackout.)*
25
26
27
28
29
30
31
32
33
34
35

Acquire U.

Summary: In this infomercial, four different women give their testimonials on how Acquire University's tape series has affected their respective lives.

Purpose: To show the emptiness of a materialistic lifestyle.

Time: 6-8 minutes

Tone: Lighthearted until the end

Cast: Ray — An infomercial salesman (male); Client — Four different consumers (played by same person) sharing their stories (female)

Costumes: Scarf, wig, jacket

Props/Set: Tape jackets for an audio tape series and a video tape series, lounge chairs, a table with pamphlets and books

Themes: Addictions, ambition, choices, consumerism, distractions, life, modern life, priorities

Text: "But godliness with contentment is great gain. For we brought nothing into the world, and we can take nothing out of it" (1 Timothy 6:6-7).

Notes: Between each testimonial, Ray addresses the audience. While he does so, Client turns her back to the audience and freezes. When he finishes his speeches, he remains facing the audience, but freezes mid-step (for example, pointing at the audience and smiling), while she delivers her next mini-monolog. If you have the multimedia capability, you could flash the words "Desire," "Acquire," "Retire," and "Expire" on a screen up front during the appropriate monologs.

1   ***SETTING:*** The set for an infomercial. As the lights come up, Client is
2   frozen On-stage with her back to the audience, standing next to a
3   table with a display of tapes and books. Ray enters, faces the
4   audience, and begins. Ray is dressed in a cheap polyester suit. He
5   looks like a stereotypical used-car salesman.
6
7   (Intro)
8   **RAY:** *(Addressing the audience)* **Are you searching for something**
9   **different? A change in your life? Maybe a new start? Are you**
10   **tired of the same old routines and priorities? Ready to find**
11   **your place in this world? If that's you, I've got some good**
12   **news. Acquire University's four-step program to success may**
13   **be just what you need to get out of that rut and on with your**
14   **life!**
15
16   (Desire)
17   **CLIENT #1:** *(Turning to face the audience)* **I was a successful**
18   **businesswoman. I had a good life, a great family, and a nice**
19   **job. But I decided I wanted more. So I signed up for Acquire**
20   **University's First Step — The Tape Series on Desire. And I**
21   **have to say, Acquire U. kept all its promises. Now I'm never**
22   **content. I always want more, more, more!** *(Turns her back to*
23   *the audience again. Each time she turns, she has taken on a*
24   *different personality and has a slightly different costume, like a*
25   *scarf, glasses, wig, jacket, or sweater over her shoulders.)*
26   **RAY: The secret lies in our patented Four-Step Philosophy to Life.**
27   **Most similar programs only offer one or two basic ideas to live**
28   **by, but our program is great for people of all ages because it**
29   **grows with you by giving you guidance in the toughest**
30   **decisions you'll ever face. Series #1 on Desire will convince**
31   **you how much you really deserve and how little you actually**
32   **have. Remember, you'll never want more as long as you're**
33   **content!**
34
35

1   (Acquire)

2   **CLIENT #2:** *(Turning around and taking on a new persona)* **I was**

3   **skeptical at first. I really wasn't sure if Acquire U. was for me.**

4   **But since I'd gone through the course on Desiring, I decided**

5   **to give it a try. So I signed up for Series #2 on Acquiring —**

6   **and boy has my life changed! I used to come home from work**

7   **and read to my kids — maybe play games with them —**

8   *(Enthusiastically)* **but not anymore! Now I sit and page**

9   **through catalogs or browse on-line while they watch TV ... I**

10   **used to go for long walks with my husband — we'd talk about**

11   **even the littlest things —** *(Enthusiastically)* **but not anymore!**

12   **He's too busy at work making the money we need to sustain**

13   **our lifestyle. And I'm always on the go — shopping for new**

14   **things or trying to maintain the things we already own! So we**

15   **hardly have any time for each other. But we're so into our**

16   **image and acquisition that we don't even miss that time**

17   **together!**

18   **My closets are full, my drawers are stuffed, and my garage**

19   **is packed with things I don't even want. It's great because the**

20   **program is so flexible. If your lifestyle changes, so do the**

21   **things you acquire. It really has endless possibilities. I'd have**

22   **to say, these days our whole lives revolve around acquisition!**

23   *(CLIENT turns back to audience.)*

24   **RAY: You see, with our new plan, you can get even more of the**

25   **things you don't need and won't ever use. We'll mail you**

26   **catalogs, flyers, and special offers you can't refuse. We'll fax**

27   **you daily sales opportunities and e-mail you offers you just**

28   **can't get anywhere else. Sign up now and get ten free**

29   **telemarketer calls a week for a full year, offering you vacation**

30   **packages around the world. You'll fill up your life with stuff in**

31   **no time at all, and then you'll be ready for our advanced**

32   **program. Let's hear what Sally Jones has to say ...**

33

34   (Retire)

35   **CLIENT #3:** *(Turning around as an older woman)* **Hi, I'm Sally**

1	Jones. Together with my husband, George, we're the Joneses,
2	the couple everyone is always trying to keep up with! And I
3	have to tell you, it's tough always staying ahead of everyone
4	else, setting the standard and never slipping into moderation.
5	We've been faithful students of Acquire University's courses
6	for as long as I can remember.
7	I finally signed up for the advanced program six months
8	ago. I'd learned to Desire and Acquire, and it was finally time
9	to Retire. My husband and I moved across the country and
10	started traveling all the time. We rarely see our friends or
11	family anymore, and we're always on the go! We've spent
12	more money in the last six months than we spent in the
13	previous six years. It's been great. And we've earned it! *(Turns*
14	*around with back to audience.)*
15	RAY: You're probably saying, "I already have everything I need."
16	But you don't have everything you want, now, do you? How
17	much would you expect to pay for a program that is
18	guaranteed to appeal to you regardless of your age,
19	background, or current financial status? That grows with you
20	through life and never lets you down? But wait! *(Holding up a*
21	*book)* There's more! If you order in the next thirty minutes,
22	we'll include our "Relationship Busters" book for free. This
23	three hundred-page book is packed with practical ways for
24	you to demand the life you want, even when it costs you your
25	closest friends.
26	That's right. Other similar programs offer contentment,
27	hope, or inner peace. But at Acquire U., we believe that it's
28	much more important to be distracted than satisfied. That's
29	why we've finally introduced our revolutionary new Fourth
30	Step ...
31	
32	(Expire)
33	CLIENT #4: *(Turning around again)* I'm Nancy. *(Pause)* I was still
34	in college when I signed up for Acquire U.'s program. I read
35	every book and listened to every tape set they published. I

1   followed all the guidelines, and everything they say is true.
2   Long ago I thought the things that mattered most were my
3   family, my faith, and my friends. But now that I have it all,
4   I've realized that nothing matters. Nothing. Nothing …
5 RAY: Desire more than you need! Acquire more than you want!
6   Retire to spend your money! And Expire before you have to —
7   just like Nancy did … Just three easy payments of $29.95. And
8   then you'll receive a new shipment each month for just
9   slightly more than you can afford. Less time with your family.
10   More debts than you can handle. This special offer is not
11   available in stores, so order now! Operators are standing by!
12   *(He freezes. Fadeout.)*
13
14
15
16
17
18
19
20
21
22
23
24
25
26
27
28
29
30
31
32
33
34
35

Piecing It Together

Summary: Jean stopped teaching last spring, but she doesn't really know what she wants to do next. Sue is trying to steer her away from interior decorating to something more "significant."

Purpose: To explore career choices and what it really means to be "called by God."

Time: 5-7 minutes

Tone: Serious

Cast: Jean — An ex-teacher who is looking for her calling (female); Sue — Her well-meaning but judgmental friend (female)

Props/Set: One-thousand-piece jigsaw puzzle, card table, two chairs

Themes: Calling, choices, church issues, consequences, judging, listening, meaning, prayer, questions, service, work

Text: "So I saw that there is nothing better for a man than to enjoy his work, because that is his lot. For who can bring him to see what will happen after him?" (Ecclesiastes 3:22).

Notes: As Sue and Jean are seated working on the jigsaw puzzle, allow their actions to express the conflict and goals each has — Jean is trying to piece her life together, but can't find all the right pieces. Sue wants to solve all of Jean's problems on the spot with easy, pat answers and shallow advice rather than listening to and supporting her friend.

1   *SETTING:* Jean's porch. Jean is seated and working on a jigsaw puzzle
2   when her friend Sue comes over to talk.
3
4   **SUE:** *(Miming looking through a window)* **Knock, knock!** *(Walking*
5   *through a doorway)* **Hello? Anyone home? Jean?**
6   **JEAN:** *(Calling, without looking up)* **I'm back here, on the porch!**
7   **SUE:** *(Crossing to JEAN)* **Hey, Jean. What are you working on?**
8   **JEAN: Hey, Sue! I'm trying to figure out this jigsaw puzzle, but I**
9   **must be missing some of the pieces or something. I just can't**
10   **seem to get it all together. It's frustrating!**
11   **SUE: Want some help?**
12   **JEAN: Sure.**
13   **SUE:** *(Sitting down)* **So, what are you looking for?**
14   **JEAN:** *(Thoughtfully)* **What am I looking for? Hmmm ... That's a**
15   **good question ...**
16   **SUE: Huh? I mean, what kind of pieces do you need?**
17   **JEAN: Oh, I need border pieces, especially the ones with a little**
18   **blue on the edge, see?** *(Holding up a piece)*
19   **SUE: Oh, OK.** *(Searching for the piece)* **So ...** *(JEAN works on the*
20   *puzzle without looking up.)* **So ... we had our first in-service**
21   **training yesterday for school this year ...**
22   **JEAN:** *(Looking at her puzzle)* **Oh, yeah ... It's about that time**
23   **again, isn't it?**
24   **SUE: I was surprised you weren't there. Everyone was.**
25   **JEAN: Yeah, a couple weeks ago I decided not to teach this year. I**
26   **hadn't really told anyone, just the principal.**
27   **SUE: Oh.**
28   **JEAN:** *(Finding a piece and talking to it)* **Aha! Thought you could**
29   **hide from me, huh? You go right over here!**
30   **SUE: So what are you gonna be doing?**
31   **JEAN: I don't know. Look for a new job, I guess.**
32   **SUE: You don't have anything lined up yet?**
33   **JEAN: Not yet.**
34   **SUE: Oh.** *(After an awkward pause)* **So ... why'd you quit?**
35   **JEAN:** *(Sighing)* **I used to think I wanted to teach. I really did. But**

1   after last spring, I guess I just decided I needed a break.

2 SUE: Rough year last year, huh?

3 JEAN: Well, yes and no. I mean ... yeah, it was kinda rough, but

4   not really that different from the other two years.

5 SUE: So?

6 JEAN: So I think maybe I'm just not cut out to be a teacher.

7 SUE: *(Handing her a piece)* Here's one with blue on it.

8 JEAN: Oh, good. I needed that one.

9 SUE: But you're a good teacher.

10 JEAN: Maybe I am ... I don't know ...

11 SUE: *(Locating a piece and fitting it into place)* So what do you think

12   you're gonna do now?

13 JEAN: Well, I don't know. I was thinking about interior decorating.

14 SUE: Interior decorating? Oh.

15 JEAN: Yeah, that's been my reaction, too.

16 SUE: What do you mean?

17 JEAN: Well, it's been kind of a tough decision, you know: touching

18   kids' lives forever or redesigning people's closets.

19 SUE: Yeah.

20 JEAN: So I'm not really sure.

21 SUE: Have you prayed about it?

22 JEAN: Yeah.

23 SUE: And what does God say?

24 JEAN: Nothing. No signs from heaven yet. That's the thing — I

25   don't really know what he wants me to do. I'm kind of in

26   limbo.

27 SUE: Well, don't you think it'd be better to wait for some direction

28   before abandoning your career?

29 JEAN: You're my friend. You're supposed to be supporting me!

30 SUE: But I don't understand. You went to college to become a

31   teacher, you jumped through all the hoops, you landed a good

32   job in a really nice school district —

33 JEAN: But I didn't enjoy teaching.

34 SUE: I thought you loved kids.

35 JEAN: I do! I just don't know if teaching is right for me. I don't

1   think it's my … calling.

2   SUE: Well, what *is* your calling?

3   JEAN: *(Working at the puzzle)* I don't know. All I know is that I

4   didn't really feel at peace teaching.

5   SUE: Everyone has a part of their job they don't enjoy —

6   JEAN: I know that! *(Getting frustrated at the puzzle)* This stupid

7   puzzle! I just don't seem to have all the pieces!

8   SUE: *(After a pause)* So what does an interior decorator do?

9   JEAN: Well, you go into people's homes and decorate — you know,

10   coordinating the carpet with the drapes, making everything

11   look prettier, more homey, things like that.

12   SUE: Well, maybe God can use you to witness to someone when you

13   visit their home.

14   JEAN: Is that the only reason to get a job?

15   SUE: Well, no —

16   JEAN: It doesn't seem very genuine, does it? Like, get a job so that

17   you might run into someone who might not know God and

18   maybe you can witness to them? Doesn't that seem more like

19   an ulterior motive than a calling?

20   SUE: But —

21   JEAN: I'm serious. How do you know if you're where God wants

22   you to be?

23   SUE: Jean, the most important thing is to serve God.

24   JEAN: Can't I serve him as an interior decorator?

25   SUE: I guess, but don't you want to do something a little more

26   *significant* with your life?

27   JEAN: Significant, huh? Isn't it important to do something I

28   enjoy? *(Freeze. Fadeout.)*

29

30

31

32

33

34

35

Part 2
Modern
Moral Dilemmas

Jesus never turned his back on the difficult issues of his day. He faced them head-on — in his preaching, teaching, and storytelling. Jesus addressed issues such as unforgiveness, racism, extortion, hypocrisy, complacency, lust, and materialism.

And sometimes his stories were shocking. They weren't tidy little fairy tales. They left people feeling very uncomfortable. And convicted.

The sketches in this section aren't meant for every Sunday morning worship service. They tackle some pretty heavy issues. These sketches are gritty. Yet they bring up the same kind of issues Jesus addressed. And they reveal real struggles that many church-going people face today.

You may find that these sketches will work best for a special service, conference, or Bible study on a particular topic. Be sensitive to the needs of your congregation. But don't be afraid of addressing the real issues people struggle with. Jesus did it. So should we.

Date Night

Summary: Frank hasn't been close to his teenage daughter. Now that he's trying to reconnect with her, she's unsure of his motives.

Purpose: To show that reconciliation is possible, but it requires time and effort.

Time: 5-7 minutes

Tone: Serious, heartwarming

Cast: Jessica — A teenager wondering why her divorced father suddenly wants to get involved in her life again (female); Frank — A father who is trying to reconnect with his daughter (male)

Props/Set: A ring, ring box, two menus, coffee cups, table setting at a nice restaurant, glasses of water

Themes: Communication, dating, divorce, family life, love, parenting, prayer, promises, purity, relationships, second chances, sex, teenagers, temptation

Text: "For the grace of God that brings salvation has appeared to all men. It teaches us to say 'No' to ungodliness and worldly passions, and to live self-controlled, upright and godly lives in this present age" (Titus 2:11-12).

Notes: Throughout the sketch, Frank feels awkward and a little uncomfortable. Jessica is a typical (14- to 16-year-old) teenager. You could add a server if desired.

1   *SETTING:* A classy restaurant. As the scene opens, Frank and Jessica
2   are seated at a table looking over their menus.
3
4   **FRANK:** *(Unsure what to say)* **So how about a nice big juicy**
5   **cheeseburger tonight?**
6   **JESSICA: I don't eat meat, Dad. I'm a vegetarian.**
7   **FRANK: Oh ... I thought you liked cheeseburgers.**
8   **JESSICA: I did when I was a kid.**
9   **FRANK: Oh ... How about an appetizer then? Maybe some onion**
10   **rings?**
11   **JESSICA: Onion rings make you fat.**
12   **FRANK: Oh.** *(To himself)* **Onion rings make you fat. I eat onion**
13   **rings all the time.** *(She looks up at him as if to say, "See?")* **All**
14   **right ... no appetizer.**
15   **JESSICA: So, like, what are you trying to accomplish tonight?**
16   **FRANK: Um, ordering our food would be a nice start.**
17   **JESSICA: I mean, why are we here?**
18   **FRANK:** *(Trying to be funny; it doesn't work)* **'Cause I like this place.**
19   **They have good onion rings.**
20   **JESSICA:** *(Disgusted with him)* **Dad!**
21   **FRANK:** *(Finally talking from the heart)* **Jessie, I was just hoping we**
22   **could be together for a little while. Maybe talk.**
23   **JESSICA: I hardly see you for like a year, and then all of a sudden,**
24   **it's like, "Wanna meet me for dinner?" I don't get it. Why this**
25   **like sudden interest in my life?**
26   **FRANK:** *(Embarrassed to admit it)* **I, um ... I went to this conference,**
27   **and they told us to take our daughters out on a date.**
28   **JESSICA: A date?**
29   **FRANK: Yeah.**
30   **JESSICA: With your daughter?**
31   **FRANK: Uh-huh. To spend time together. To get to know each**
32   **other better. Help her feel special.**
33   **JESSICA: Oh.**
34   **FRANK:** *(Trying to get back to ordering the food)* **So what do you eat**
35   **now that you're not a kid anymore?**

1   JESSICA: Um, salad. And sometimes falafel.

2   FRANK: Falafel? What's that?

3   JESSICA: It's like this grain burger thing. It's pretty good.

4   FRANK: Oh.

5   JESSICA: So, what kind of conference was it?

6   FRANK: *(He is still looking at, and hiding behind, his menu.)* **Huh?**

7   JESSICA: The one where they told you to take your daughters on

8   a date. Was it some kind of therapy thing?

9   FRANK: Um. It was a men's conference thing. *(Pretending to*

10   *interact with a server)* Oh, uh, yeah. We'll have a Caesar salad

11   *(Looking at JESSICA for approval. She nods)* and, um, I guess

12   we'll have two of those. And *(To JESSICA)* what do you want

13   to drink?

14   JESSICA: *(To server)* Water with lemon and no ice.

15   FRANK: *(To server)* OK, and I'll have some coffee … no, just some

16   sugar. Thanks. Yeah, that's all.

17   JESSICA: You didn't have to order a salad just 'cause I did.

18   FRANK: I know. I thought I'd give it a shot. *(Patting belly)*

19   Couldn't hurt. *(To server who is pouring his coffee)* Thank you.

20   JESSICA: You shouldn't really drink that stuff. Caffeine is bad for

21   you.

22   FRANK: You don't drink coffee? I thought all teenagers drank

23   coffee these days.

24   JESSICA: Well, I don't.

25   FRANK: *(Awkwardly)* Oh … So how's your mom?

26   JESSICA: She's good, I guess. She's been seeing this guy from

27   work. He comes over like all the time.

28   FRANK: Is he nice?

29   JESSICA: He's OK. I think they're getting serious.

30   FRANK: Oh. Well, I guess that's good, then.

31   JESSICA: Yeah. So what do you do at a men's conference?

32   FRANK: You, um … well, we sang … and we listened to speakers.

33   And we … well, we prayed for our families.

34   JESSICA: You prayed for me?

35   FRANK: Yeah. I've been praying for you a lot.

1   JESSICA: I didn't know you prayed at all.
2   FRANK: I started.
3   JESSICA: Oh.
4   FRANK: I, uh, I've got something for you. *(Reaching into his pocket*
5   *and pulling out a small box with a ring in it)*
6   JESSICA: *(As she takes it)* **What is this?**
7   FRANK: Open it up.
8   JESSICA: *(She opens it and pulls out a gold ring.)* **Wow. Dad, this is**
9   **nice. It looks real.**
10   FRANK: It is.
11   JESSICA: **This musta cost a lot. What's the occasion? It's not like**
12   **my birthday or anything —**
13   FRANK: It's a ... commitment ring.
14   JESSICA: **What's that?**
15   FRANK: *(Very awkward. He's having a difficult time wording this*
16   *because he doesn't know if it's already too late to give it to her.)*
17   **It's a ring that you wear until you get married, and it's**
18   **supposed to symbolize a commitment ... to remain ... sexually**
19   **pure until then.**
20   JESSICA: **Oh. So like, if I take it, then I have to agree not to sleep**
21   **with anyone until I get married?**
22   FRANK: Well, that's the idea.
23   JESSICA: **Huh.**
24   FRANK: I don't know how to say this ... um, we haven't been
25   really close the last couple years.
26   JESSICA: *(As if she is saying "no kidding")* **Yeah?**
27   FRANK: Well ... um, I'm not really too up-to-date on your dating
28   life, but some girls your age are already —
29   JESSICA: **Oh, I get it. You're not sure if it's too late already, huh?**
30   **Like maybe you went to this conference thing, and they tell**
31   **you to buy your daughters these cool rings and then you're**
32   **like, "Well, what if my daughter's already sleeping around,**
33   **then what?" But you decided to go ahead and find out.**
34   FRANK: Yeah. That about sums it up.
35   JESSICA: **Well, it's not.**

1   FRANK: It's not what?

2   JESSICA: It's not too late.

3   FRANK: Really?

4   JESSICA: Really. Billy and I were pretty serious, but I always told

5   him I wanted to wait.

6   FRANK: I'm proud of you.

7   JESSICA: Really?

8   FRANK: Yeah. It's tough for young people growing up today.

9   There's a lot of pressure to do stuff that's not right. It takes a

10   lot of guts to say "no." It's not easy.

11   JESSICA: You're telling me. *(Admiring her ring)* Um, this ring and

12   everything, well, it's pretty cool. But can I think about it? The

13   commitment, I mean?

14   FRANK: Um. Sure.

15   JESSICA: I just wouldn't want to say "yes" and make that kind of

16   promise unless I was pretty sure I could keep it.

17   FRANK: I understand.

18   JESSICA: So can I wear it until I decide?

19   FRANK: Yeah.

20   JESSICA: Which finger is it supposed to go on? *(She slips it on her*

21   *ring finger.)*

22   FRANK: Yeah, that one. Wow, Jessie. It looks great on you … Hey!

23   Here comes our salad!

24   JESSICA: Good … Um, do you think we could do this again

25   sometime?

26   FRANK: *(Smirking)* Are you asking me out for another date?

27   JESSICA: Yeah.

28   FRANK: You mean you're not embarrassed being on a date with

29   your old man?

30   JESSICA: No … *(Shyly)* Are you embarrassed to be seen with me?

31   FRANK: *(Tenderly)* Not at all.

32   JESSICA: Even if I order falafel?

33   FRANK: Naw. As long as I can have some onion rings.

34   JESSICA: Deal. *(She reaches out her hand, FRANK takes it and they*

35   *shake. She smiles.)* So is that a "yes"?

1   **FRANK:** Yeah, it's a "yes." It's a very big yes … *(FRANK rests her*
2   *hand on the table, and while he is still holding it, they freeze.*
3   *Fadeout.)*
4
5
6
7
8
9
10
11
12
13
14
15
16
17
18
19
20
21
22
23
24
25
26
27
28
29
30
31
32
33
34
35

Clean Hands

Summary: Janet can't stop blaming herself for her daughter's death. But when Andrew tries to help, he realizes he doesn't have any answers either.

Purpose: To demonstrate the futility of trying to deal with guilt on our own, apart from God.

Time: 4-6 minutes

Tone: Serious

Cast: Janet — A hurting and alienated woman consumed with guilt (female); Andrew — Her concerned, yet unable-to-help husband (male)

Props/Set: Water, soap, sponge, dish towel, a wash basin, tub or sink with dishes

Themes: Coping, death, family life, forgiveness, God's power, guilt, parenting, questions, regrets, sin, suffering

Text: "You are already clean because of the word I have spoken to you" (John 15:3).

Notes: In this sketch, neither person has any real answers; neither one knows God. Use this sketch to set up a message on dealing with guilt or accepting forgiveness.

1   *SETTING:* The kitchen after supper. Dishes are piled high. As the
2   scene opens, Janet is On-stage washing the dishes. After a few
3   moments, she begins washing her arms and mumbling to herself,
4   staring past her hands into space.
5
6   JANET: *(To herself)* I can't wash it off ... I can't get it off ...
7   ANDREW: *(Entering)* Hey, Janet! Want some help with the dishes?
8   How about you wash and I dry? *(Picking up a towel and a plate,*
9   *he notices she is scrubbing her arms.)* What are you doing?
10 JANET: *(Not noticing him)* I can't wash it off!
11 ANDREW: Wash what off? Janet?
12 JANET: *(Still not looking up)* The blood! It's all over my hands.
13 ANDREW: Blood?! *(Taking her hands and turning her arms so that*
14   *he can see them)* You don't have any blood on your hands.
15 JANET: *(Still staring off into space)* Yes, I do! I have to get it off.
16 ANDREW: Janet! Your hands are clean!
17 JANET: *(Shaking her head "no")* Hannah's blood is all over them.
18 ANDREW: Hannah's blood?
19 JANET: My daughter's blood!
20 ANDREW: I know who Hannah was.
21 JANET: She's dead.
22 ANDREW: I know.
23 JANET: I killed her.
24 ANDREW: You didn't kill her.
25 JANET: Yes I did.
26 ANDREW: Her death was not your fault!
27 JANET: *(Finally, she makes eye contact with ANDREW.)* I was
28   driving the car! I hit the telephone pole! Who else's fault could
29   it be? One minute she's sleeping peacefully in the backseat
30   and I'm smiling at her in the rear view mirror. And the next
31   minute I'm spilling the coffee and swerving and sliding and
32   then ... and then it's too late ... I tried to help her. I really did.
33   But her blood got on my arms ... I have to get it off!
34 ANDREW: I know all about the accident. You don't have to remind
35   me! But Hannah died four years ago ... No one blames you for

1   her death.

2   JANET: Don't you?

3   ANDREW: No ... I mean ... there's nothing we can do about it

4   now. So I guess you just gotta try and forget about it and move

5   on. All right?

6   JANET: I can't forget about it. I was driving the car when it

7   crashed!

8   ANDREW: Yeah, you were driving the car. But it was just as much

9   my fault. I mean, I was too drunk to stand up that night

10   anyhow. It might have been me behind the wheel —

11   JANET: But it wasn't you. It was me. It was my fault. *(Staring off*

12   *into space again)* I still see her ... *(Turning back to the sink)* I

13   have to wash this off. If I can only clean my —

14   ANDREW: Janet, you're scaring me. I thought we went through all

15   this already. I thought you were over it! We all make mistakes.

16   JANET: My mistake was forever.

17   ANDREW: *(Reaching over and physically turning her head so he can*

18   *look directly into her eyes)* Listen to me. I blew it, too. Every

19   time I see a little girl, I remember how I always had an excuse

20   for not spending more time with Hannah. I remember how

21   she'd ask me to read her books, and I'd say, "Later, honey,

22   when I'm done with the paper." But later never came. *(Letting*

23   *go of her)*

24   JANET: And it's not just the accident. Deep down I know I'm not

25   what I should be ...

26   ANDREW: And how badly she wanted me to come to her

27   kindergarten dance recital, but I missed it because I was

28   passed out on the couch ...

29   JANET: ... And the harder I try to do what's right, the more lost I

30   feel ...

31   ANDREW: I was killing her off, little by little.

32   JANET: *(Scrubbing her arms again)* How can I wash this off? I just

33   can't seem to get myself clean.

34   ANDREW: *(Shaking off his moment of reflection)* Look. Maybe you

35   should go see that shrink again or something.

1   JANET: He didn't help. I couldn't get rid of the guilt. He told me
2   to just look inside myself for the answers. But I'm too filled
3   with hurt inside. I don't have any answers.
4   ANDREW: *(Starting to get angry)* You think I do? I don't have any
5   answers either! But you don't see me blaming myself, feeling
6   guilty. You just gotta tell yourself it doesn't matter —
7   JANET: That's what the counselor said. But it does matter. I know
8   it does.
9   ANDREW: No! You have to tell yourself it doesn't matter. It's the
10   only way —
11   JANET: Then I wouldn't be filled with hurt, I'd be filled with
12   emptiness.
13   ANDREW: *(Becoming more contemplative as he realizes she is right)*
14   Maybe you need to talk to a priest or a rabbi or something.
15   JANET: *(Hopefully)* Do you think that would help? I thought you
16   didn't believe in God.
17   ANDREW: I don't … I mean, how should I know? Maybe there is
18   a god, maybe not … It'd be easier if there was. At least then
19   there'd be someone to blame — someone besides ourselves …
20   *(More to himself than to her)* Sometimes I wish there was …
21   JANET: *(Begins to wash her hands again)* I'll get this off. I just need
22   to scrub a little harder. Gimme a little more time. I'll get it off.
23   I have to. *(Freeze. Blackout.)*
24
25
26
27
28
29
30
31
32
33
34
35

Getting the Last Word

Summary: Kyle is finally ready to tell his father how much he loves him. But has he waited too long?

Purpose: To show the importance of valuing our family members while we still have the chance.

Time: 4-6 minutes

Tone: Serious

Cast: Kyle — A 35-year-old man who has waited too long to tell his father he loves him (male); Timmy — His 11-year-old son (male)

Props/Set: A bouquet of flowers, hand-held video game, briefcase, two park benches

Themes: Choices, communication, family life, love, parenting, regrets, relationships

Text: "But encourage one another daily, as long as it is called Today" (Hebrews 3:13a).

Notes: Often people wait until it's too late to show how much they care about someone else. This sketch will help set up a message on family life, especially relationships between fathers and sons. At the beginning, Kyle should pretend that he's actually talking to his father. He is trying to say "I love you," but it isn't easy. Timmy is tired of waiting for his dad and wants to get going.

1   ***SETTING:*** A graveyard — but don't give this away. The impact of this
2   sketch comes at the end, when the audience finally realizes that
3   Kyle is not talking to his father in person, but only his dad's
4   tombstone. As the scene opens, Kyle is seated on a park bench and
5   Timmy is Off-stage.
6
7   **KYLE: Well, Dad, I don't really know how to say this …** *(Mumbling*
8   *to himself)* **Right …** *(To his dad)* **Hey, I saw the Brewers game**
9   **last night on TV — they won by three runs! Yeah … I**
10   **remember back when I was a kid, you used to take me to the**
11   **ballpark to see the Brewers play. We'd get there early and set**
12   **up that little portable grill of yours in the parking lot … Grill**
13   **some hot dogs and burgers there before the game. Yeah …**
14   **Tailgate parties. That's what you called them.** *(Chuckling a*
15   *little)* **Those were good times …**
16   **There was that one time in the fifth grade when Josh**
17   **Remington spent the night and then the next morning you**
18   **took us to the stadium for a doubleheader … We had that**
19   **burping contest in the parking lot after chugging cans of 7-Up.**
20   **Man, Josh thought I was so cool to have an old man who could**
21   **burp with the best of 'em. His dad had left him like two years**
22   **earlier or something like that. I'd never really thought of it**
23   **before then, but yeah, it was pretty cool …**
24   **We used to go camping, remember that? We'd sit in that**
25   **tiny little tent and you'd tell me scary stories until I almost wet**
26   **my sleeping bag, and then we'd just start telling stupid jokes**
27   **and stay up until the middle of the night laughing our heads**
28   **off. You taught me how to do all that cool knot-tying Boy**
29   **Scout stuff. Not that I remember any of it anymore …**
30   *(Melodramatically)* **And then came high school. Yikes! I**
31   **wasn't exactly your model kid growing up … especially my**
32   **junior year … and then going to tech school … and moving**
33   **away … I know we haven't really been that close the last**
34   **couple of years. I don't really know what happened. It was**
35   **like one day we just stopped talking and never really picked it**

1   up again …
2   I know you didn't approve of the divorce — hey, that's up
3   to you. But I was a jerk to make such a big deal about getting
4   you to understand it all and support me. I know you and Mom
5   were married for like thirty years or thirty-five or whatever.
6   But it just didn't work out with Timmy's mom and me … I
7   don't know, I feel kinda stupid spouting all this out here
8   today, but it's been bottled up and I didn't wanna put it off
9   any longer. I hope you can understand that I'm sorry I didn't
10   say it all sooner … *(TIMMY enters.)*
11   TIMMY: Hey dad, are you coming? I've been sitting in the car
12   forever.
13   KYLE: *(Looking over at TIMMY)* Yeah, just a minute, Timmy. Um …
14   I'll be right there. *(TIMMY sits down on a park bench and starts*
15   *playing a hand-held video game. KYLE leans over and delivers*
16   *the next set of lines in a lowered, whispering voice.)* I'm taking
17   the kid to the ballgame tonight. It's not the Brewers or
18   anything, just some local semi-pro team, but I thought maybe
19   we'd grill some hot dogs out in the parking lot before the
20   game … Maybe chug some sodas … I know it's a little late for
21   this … but I wanted you to know that … *(Pause)* I do … I love
22   you, Dad. I wish I would have told you sooner … I'm sorry.
23   *(Reaches into his briefcase and pulls out some flowers, lays them*
24   *on the ground, stands up, and then joins TIMMY.)*
25   TIMMY: Who were you talking to, Dad?
26   KYLE: Oh, no one.
27   TIMMY: *(Looking around uneasily)* Graveyards sure are creepy
28   places.
29   KYLE: Yeah. C'mon, we'd better hurry or we'll be late for the
30   game. *(Freeze. Fadeout.)*
31
32
33
34
35

None of Your Business

Summary: Brett Davis thought he was safe with a small "indiscretion," but he is about to find out that all choices have consequences.

Purpose: To show that integrity is a way of life, not something you can turn on and off.

Time: 3-5 minutes

Tone: Serious

Cast: Brett Davis — A sly and conniving chief financial officer (male); Mr. Hutch — His morally conscious boss (male)

Props/Set: Telephone, two mugs of coffee, a laptop computer, two office chairs — one behind the desk and one in front of it, large oak desk with papers

Themes: Adultery, ambition, assumptions, choices, consequences, dating, excuses, integrity, lust, modern life, obedience, purity, temptation, trust, truth, work

Text: "The integrity of the upright guides them, but the unfaithful are destroyed by their duplicity" (Proverbs 11:3).

Notes: Both actors should be dressed in nice suits. Be sure that the stage is set so that they're able to remain open to (i.e., facing) the audience while they carry on their conversation with each other.

1   *SETTING:* An elite corporate office. As the scene opens, Mr. Hutch is
2   seated behind the desk. Brett Davis is Off-stage.
3

4   **HUTCH:** *(Pressing an intercom button on the telephone and speaking*
5   *into it)* **All right, Miss Baker. Send him in.**
6   **DAVIS:** *(Entering with a cocky smile on his face)* **You wanted to see**
7   **me, sir?**
8   **HUTCH:** *(Rising to greet DAVIS)* **Yes, Davis, c'mon in. Have a seat.**
9   *(Motions to the empty chair.)* **Would you like some coffee?**
10   **DAVIS:** **No thanks ... Hey, did you see the Pacers game last night?**
11   *(Or insert name of a local sports team.)* **They really pulled it out**
12   **in the last couple minutes. I was sure they were toast when —**
13   **HUTCH:** *(Interrupting DAVIS's small talk)* **Let me cut to the chase.**
14   **I'm not one to beat around the bush, so I'm just gonna come**
15   **out and say it. The word around the office is you've been**
16   **spending a little extracurricular time with Ms. Anderson, the**
17   **consultant we called in for the Baker proposal.**
18   **DAVIS:** *(Relieved)* **Beth? You called me in about Beth? Oh, sir. I**
19   **gotta say, at first when I heard you wanted to see me, I**
20   **thought maybe there was a problem or something!** *(Whew)*
21   **You had me going there! Yeah, Beth ... We got together a few**
22   **times for a drink. No big deal.**
23   **HUTCH:** **Yes, well, Ms. Anderson got a call yesterday from a very**
24   **irate woman who said she was your wife. Apparently you told**
25   **Ms. Anderson that you're divorced.**
26   **DAVIS:** *(Still trying to cover his tracks)* **Yeah, well ... I mean, you**
27   **gotta keep your options open.** *(Winking and hinting)* **You know**
28   **how the game is played —**
29   **HUTCH:** **Just so I'm clear about this — why exactly did you take**
30   **an attractive, intelligent, single woman out for a date and tell**
31   **her you're divorced when you're not?**
32   **DAVIS:** *(After a pause)* **Well, you know ... I was just trying to have**
33   **a good time, see what developed ...** *(No response from HUTCH)*
34   **C'mon, you gotta be kidding me, right? I gotta say, I'm a little**
35   **surprised you're even bringing this up. I mean, my private life**

1   is my private life.
2   HUTCH: Ms. Anderson was quite offended when she found out
3   you're still married. She quit the account, Davis. Now, she was
4   a good consultant — reliable and trustworthy.
5   DAVIS: *(A little uneasy)* I'm sorry to hear that she's no longer with
6   us, sir. But what does that have to do with me?
7   HUTCH: Well, Davis, I just lost a good consultant and my chief
8   financial officer in the same day.
9   DAVIS: *(Shocked)* What are you talking about? I'm your chief
10   financial officer!
11   HUTCH: What are our core values, Davis? Read them to me from
12   the plaque on the wall over there.
13   DAVIS: Service. Value. Integrity. Trust.
14   HUTCH: I believe in those values, Davis —
15   DAVIS: Listen, it was nothing! We didn't have an affair, we didn't
16   sleep together. Nothing! We just had a few laughs!
17   HUTCH: Do you know how many of those core values you broke
18   by having a few laughs?
19   DAVIS: *(Really nervous)* Sir —
20   HUTCH: All of them. Service, because we lost a good consultant.
21   Value, because that costs us money. Integrity, because you lied
22   to Ms. Anderson, hoping to seduce her. And trust, because
23   now I no longer trust you — and by the way, neither should
24   your wife. I can't have someone I don't trust in charge of my
25   company's finances, now can I, Davis?
26   DAVIS: You're blowing this all out of proportion! We are talking
27   about my private life here!
28   HUTCH: Integrity has no private life, Davis.
29   DAVIS: But you've seen my work! My reports! The audits!
30   Everything's in order! I've never been dishonest in my job in
31   any way!
32   HUTCH: Yes, I've seen your work. But character isn't how you act
33   when I'm looking over your shoulder. It's how you act when
34   I'm not.
35   DAVIS: My personal life is none of your business!

1   HUTCH: This business is my business. My consultants are my
2   business. Those core values are my business. And my finances
3   are definitely my business. But you're right, Mr. Davis. Your
4   private life is no longer any of my business. Good-bye.
5   DAVIS: But —
6   HUTCH: Good-bye, Davis. That'll be all. *(After a beat, blackout.)*

7
8
9
10
11
12
13
14
15
16
17
18
19
20
21
22
23
24
25
26
27
28
29
30
31
32
33
34
35

Life Sentence

Summary: When his sister was killed seven years ago, Alan decided he would never forgive her murderer. But now that the man is about to be executed, Alan must decide if he should keep hating him or finally forgive him.

Purpose: To show how resentment and unforgiveness can imprison us.

Time: 6-8 minutes

Tone: Serious

Cast: Alan Sundquist — A bitter man whose sister was killed (male); Lawrence Kincaid — The death-row inmate who shot her (male)

Costume: Orange jumpsuit for Kincaid

Props/Set: Handcuffs, wristwatch, table, two chairs

Themes: Consequences, death penalty, forgiveness, grudges, hatred, regrets, resentment

Text: "For if you forgive men when they sin against you, your heavenly Father will also forgive you. But if you do not forgive men their sins, your Father will not forgive your sins" (Matthew 6:14-15).

Notes: When Alan finally tells Kincaid that he forgives him, it should be a moment when the audience is on his side. Then, as he realizes that he was only being selfish in his "forgiveness," those in the audience should be asking themselves, "Then what *does* it mean to forgive someone?" Let the table be the focal point for the action. They can lean across it, stand near it, sit beside it, or pound on it as they talk.

1   *SETTING:* The visiting room of a maximum security prison. As the
2   lights come up, we see Kincaid seated behind the table. He is
3   wearing an orange jumpsuit and has handcuffs on. Alan mimes
4   opening a door as he enters the visiting room.
5
6   ALAN: Hi.
7   KINCAID: Hi.
8   ALAN: So. *(KINCAID is silent.)* Um. I'm not really sure what to say.
9   *(Again, KINCAID is silent.)* Right. *(Sighs.)*
10   KINCAID: You're the one who wanted to see me.
11   ALAN: Yeah, I wanted to meet you.
12   KINCAID: Why?
13   ALAN: *(Coldly)* You remember the lady in the gas station? The one
14   who showed up in the middle of the robbery? That was my
15   sister.
16   KINCAID: *(Leaning forward)* Your sister?
17   ALAN: Yeah. You killed her. You shot her in the chest and then let
18   her bleed to death on the floor.
19   KINCAID: And so you came to see me —
20   ALAN: Yeah.
21   KINCAID: After all this time.
22   ALAN: Yeah.
23   KINCAID: Why? To gloat? Because the day you've been looking
24   forward to is almost here?
25   ALAN: No, I needed to ask you something.
26   KINCAID: What's that?
27   ALAN: Did you lie?
28   KINCAID: When?
29   ALAN: At the trial.
30   KINCAID: No.
31   ALAN: Are you sure?
32   KINCAID: Yeah! I'm no liar! It was true. Everything I said was
33   true. I freaked out and fired the gun when the door opened. I
34   didn't want to shoot anyone. What's this all about?
35   ALAN: Are you sorry?

1   KINCAID: What — are you kidding me? Of course I'm sorry! I've
2   spent a fourth of my life locked up because your sister didn't
3   make it!
4   ALAN: I don't mean just because you got caught. I mean, do you
5   even care that she's dead?
6   KINCAID: Yeah, I care. I do! *(Silence from ALAN)* Listen, I know
7   it's gotta be rough for you — your sister getting killed like that
8   and all. But there's nothing I can say that'll bring her back …
9   It's been seven years.
10   ALAN: I know.
11   KINCAID: It's a little late for all this, isn't it? I mean, you do know
12   what's scheduled to happen to me next week, don't you?
13   ALAN: Yeah, I do. That's why I finally came.
14   KINCAID: Wait a minute … was my testimony true … am I sorry …
15   what are you getting at?
16   ALAN: I also needed to tell you something.
17   KINCAID: What's that?
18   ALAN: For a long time I hated you for what you did.
19   KINCAID: I would have hated me, too.
20   ALAN: No, I mean, I *really* hated you. I wanted you dead. I was
21   looking forward to your execution. I would've pushed the
22   syringe into your arm myself if they would've let me.
23   KINCAID: Is that what you came to say?
24   ALAN: No. Here goes … *(Searching for the words)* I can't say it …
25   KINCAID: Can't say what?
26   ALAN: OK … *(Taking a deep breath)* I forgive you.
27   KINCAID: You forgive me?
28   ALAN: Yeah. I forgive you.
29   KINCAID: And?
30   ALAN: And that's it. That's all. That's what I came to say. I forgive
31   you for shooting my sister.
32   KINCAID: OK, *(Pausing and leaning forward expectantly)* so now
33   what? Should I call my lawyers or something?
34   ALAN: Why?
35   KINCAID: For the stay of execution!

1   ALAN: What are you talking about?

2   KINCAID: I'm supposed to be executed next week —

3   ALAN: Yeah. And?

4   KINCAID: And you come in here asking me if I'm sorry for

5   shooting her, and then you tell me I'm forgiven! Why should

6   I die if you forgive me? If you really forgive me for what I did,

7   why should I be punished for it? We can work this all out —

8   ALAN: Wait a minute. I didn't come here for that. You're getting

9   what you deserve.

10   KINCAID: What? I thought you just said you forgave me.

11   ALAN: I did. I mean, I do.

12   KINCAID: Then what kind of a game are you playing? You come

13   in here acting all nice to get my hopes up and then just dash

14   them again?

15   ALAN: For seven years I hated you. For seven years I wanted you

16   dead.

17   KINCAID: Yeah, you said that.

18   ALAN: Well, you were sentenced by a judge for what you did.

19   KINCAID: So?

20   ALAN: I was sentencing myself for what you did. I realized my

21   time was running out.

22   KINCAID: How do you figure? I'm the one getting killed!

23   ALAN: If I didn't forgive you, I'd be carrying all that anger

24   around forever. I'd be bitter and resentful. Most people never

25   take the time to forgive someone. They bury the anger down

26   deep and wait, thinking the day will come when they'll finally

27   say those words. And that unforgiveness festers and grows,

28   and then when the person they're angry at moves away or

29   dies, it's too late. They have to live with that regret forever. I

30   didn't want to live like that.

31   KINCAID: So let me get this straight. You came in here to tell me

32   you forgive me just because you wanted to *feel better*?!

33   ALAN: *(Suddenly uneasy)* No, I —

34   KINCAID: Yeah, that's it! That's what you just said! You don't

35   really forgive me!

1   ALAN: What do you mean?

2   KINCAID: You're just afraid of having to live with all that hatred

3   for the rest of your life. You just don't want to have to feel

4   guilty after I'm gone! You're just like me —

5   ALAN: *(Angrily)* What are you talking about?

6   KINCAID: I never cared about your sister! I'm just sorry I got

7   caught.

8   ALAN: What?!

9   KINCAID: And you never cared about me, you just felt sorry for

10   yourself. That's why you came here! And now, once I'm dead,

11   you can pat yourself on the back and tell yourself what a great

12   guy you are. That's not forgiveness!

13   ALAN: Oh, yeah? Then forget it! *(Leaning close to KINCAID)* I

14   *don't* forgive you, then! OK?! *(To Off-stage)* Guard, let me out!

15   I'm finished in here.

16   KINCAID: So you don't forgive me now?!

17   ALAN: *(Angrily)* I wasn't gonna be there. I really wasn't. But now

18   you can count on it. I'm gonna be sitting in that room

19   watching. I'll see you next week, Lawrence Kincaid. *(Exits.)*

20   KINCAID: *(Standing up and laughing)* See? You still hate me! You

21   are like me! Only difference is, for me it ends next week! Did

22   you hear me? For me it ends next week! *(Freeze. Blackout.)*

23

24

25

26

27

28

29

30

31

32

33

34

35

Reunion

Summary: John returns home two months after having an affair, and Amy isn't sure how to respond. She wants to forgive him and start over, but how?

Purpose: To reveal the consequences of sin and the real-life difficulties of forgiveness.

Time: 5-7 minutes

Tone: Serious

Cast: John — A repentant husband who has been unfaithful to his wife (male); Amy — His hardworking wife who is trying to forgive him (female)

Props/Set: Suitcase, vacuum cleaner, couch

Themes: Adultery, choices, consequences, family life, forgiveness, grace, guilt, home, married life, promises, regrets, relationships, repentance, second chances, sex, sin, temptation

Text: "If we confess our sins, he is faithful and just and will forgive us our sins and purify us from all unrighteousness" (1 John 1:9).

Notes: Forgiving others for deep wounds is often a process rather than a single event. It usually takes time and requires a conscious decision to continue forgiving. This sketch shows that being willing to forgive is the first step in the process. When directing this scene, be sensitive to the movement and actions of the characters so they don't just stand around giving each other speeches. Use the couch to your advantage, and let John and Amy sit or stand as the sketch develops.

1   *SETTING:* Amy's living room. The stage is bare except for a couch.
2   As the scene opens, Amy is vacuuming the carpet and
3   straightening the couch cushions. John enters carrying a suitcase.
4   He sets it down and Amy turns to see him. Amy is surprised and
5   caught off-guard at first.
6
7   **AMY:** *(Very surprised and taken aback to see him)* **John?**
8   **JOHN: Amy.**
9   **AMY:** *(After a pause)* **You're back —**
10   **JOHN: Yeah.**
11   **TOGETHER: Look, I —**
12   **JOHN: You go first.**
13   **AMY:** *(Edgy)* **No, you.**
14   **JOHN: Uh, how are the kids?**
15   **AMY:** *(Kind of in shock)* **The kids.** *(Quickly)* **Well, Andy has a sore**
16   **throat. I think it's from his soccer game the other day; it**
17   **rained the whole time. And Joey, he's good, although his**
18   **grades have been slipping a little and he lost his glasses the**
19   **other day at school ... He placed fourth in his karate**
20   **tournament.**
21   **JOHN: That's good.**
22   **AMY: Yeah.**
23   **JOHN: And how are you?**
24   **AMY: Good. Good. I'm good, I guess. I'm doing well, considering ...**
25   **JOHN: Amy, I'm sorry.**
26   **AMY: You're sorry ...** *(Becoming emotional and upset as she repeats*
27   *the words)* **You're sorry ... Well, I'm glad you're sorry. But it's**
28   **a little late to be sorry, don't you think?**
29   **JOHN: Amy, don't start.**
30   **AMY:** *(Building to a yell)* **Don't start! Now he tells me don't start!**
31   **You come walking back in here after two months, asking**
32   **about the kids as if nothing has happened, and you tell me**
33   **"don't *start*"?**
34   **JOHN: Amy —**
35   **AMY: I'm left alone with two confused boys who think their father**

1   hates them! I'm supposed to be working *and* be their mom
2   *and* their dad — and what am I supposed to tell them when
3   they ask about their father who never writes or calls? That he
4   loves them so much he decided to move away to live with
5   someone young enough to be his daughter?
6   JOHN: Amy —
7   AMY: *(Yelling)* Don't "Amy" me! *(Quieter, but with an edge)* How is
8   what's-her-name? Marcie? Margie?
9   JOHN: Maggie.
10   AMY: *(Sarcastically)* Maggie! I don't know why I couldn't
11   remember that! How could I forget? It must be my old age!
12   I'll bet Maggie doesn't have any trouble remembering things.
13   Not like me. How old is Maggie again? Is she out of high
14   school?
15   JOHN: Amy, it's over. I came back to say I'm sorry.
16   AMY: Well, I'm sorry too, John. I'm very sorry. I'm sorry about
17   what happened, and I'm sorry you drove all the way over here
18   for nothing. Now, please get out.
19   JOHN: Amy —
20   AMY: Get out!
21   JOHN: I was hoping you could forgive me.
22   AMY: *(Shocked that he would suggest that)* Forgive you? How could
23   you expect me to forgive you? How? How! After what you
24   did!
25   JOHN: I wasn't expecting it — just hoping for it.
26   AMY: *(Quieting down, but speaking very coldly)* You've said what
27   you came to say. Now, good-bye. I have two boys to pick up
28   from school.
29   JOHN: Listen. I've been doing a lot of thinking — about you and
30   the kids.
31   AMY: *(Sarcastically)* Well, that's good.
32   JOHN: I've come to realize how special you are. I know how wrong
33   it was for me to do what I did.
34   AMY: *(Sarcastically)* Yeah, right.
35   JOHN: Please — let me finish. I know it may be too late. I know it

1   would take a lot of work, you and me, but I'd do it. I'd do

2   anything to make it work. I am so sorry. That's what I needed

3   to say. *(Picking up suitcase)* If you want me to leave now, I will.

4   AMY: *(Long pause before answering)* Why John? Why? Why did

5   you do it?

6   JOHN: *(Awkwardly, searching)* I don't have any good reasons. I

7   wasn't trying to hurt you or the boys ... I never stopped loving

8   you ... It was like I started down a wrong road and I couldn't

9   turn around. Until yesterday.

10   AMY: What happened yesterday?

11   JOHN: I was jogging, and I went past this church. There was all

12   kinds of traffic — people going to an evening service or

13   something. I had to jog in place while all these cars went into

14   the parking lot. And for some reason, I started thinking about

15   how long it had been since I'd been in a church. And then I

16   remembered the words you yelled at me when I left.

17   AMY: You heard them?

18   JOHN: Yeah, even through the door. Because I stood there for a

19   minute, trying to decide if I should really leave or not. And you

20   said, "John, I love you. Don't do this. For God's sake, don't do

21   this!" That's what you said: "For God's sake, don't do this."

22   AMY: I remember.

23   JOHN: Yeah, well yesterday, so did I. I'd never thought about those

24   words much before — you know, "for God's sake." But

25   yesterday I realized I hadn't been doing anything for God at

26   all. It was all for me. Not his sake, just mine.

27   AMY: And?

28   JOHN: And I realized I was hurting God — breaking his heart, you

29   know. And I asked myself, "How can I live like this and call

30   myself a Christian?" And then I thought of how much pain I

31   caused you and the boys. I started crying right there by that

32   church's parking lot. The people driving by must have

33   thought I was nuts. Over and over I begged God to forgive me.

34   AMY: Did he?

35   JOHN: Yeah, he did. I felt different — more at peace, you know,

1   deep down inside. For the first time since all this started, I was
2   at peace. I said good-bye to Maggie, and I drove all night and
3   here I am. I knew I had to come here today and try to make
4   things right, even if you wouldn't have me back. I hope you
5   can find it in your heart to forgive me.
6   AMY: *(No longer angry, but still unsure)* Oh, John … I don't know
7   what to say. As much as I've been hurting, I've been hoping
8   and praying for this day. But now that you're here, I … I wish
9   I could say I forgive you. I wish I could say I can forget it all.
10   But it's so sudden. Here you are today. Will you be here
11   tomorrow? I don't know what to say … I need more time.
12   *(Pausing to think)* Where are you staying?
13   JOHN: Uh, I don't know yet. I haven't had a chance to get a room.
14   I was hoping maybe … I could stay here …
15   AMY: John, no. I can't. Not yet.
16   JOHN: OK.
17   AMY: It'll take time …
18   JOHN: Yeah.
19   AMY: But I know the boys would like to see you. How about
20   finding a hotel room and then coming over for supper?
21   JOHN: Really?
22   AMY: Yeah.
23   JOHN: OK. Thanks.
24   AMY: I'm not making any promises.
25   JOHN: I know.
26   AMY: But it is good to see you.
27   JOHN: It's good to see you, too. *(They awkwardly reach to hug, but*
28   *then pull back and shake hands. As their fingers touch, fadeout.)*
29
30
31
32
33
34
35

Invisible Chains

Summary: Mark has been downloading pornography off the Internet. His wife finds out and confronts him, but then discovers she's not as innocent as she thought.

Purpose: To show how lust destroys trust and relationships.

Time: 4-6 minutes

Tone: Serious

Cast: Susie — A wife who longs for marital intimacy (female); Mark — Her husband, who is addicted to pornography (male)

Props/Set: Cooking utensils, a tray of cookies, pots, pans, countertop, a small television with soap operas on in the background

Themes: Addictions, adultery, communication, divisiveness, excuses, hiding, lust, married life, pornography, purity, running away, secrets, sex, sin, trust

Text: "You have heard that it was said, 'Do not commit adultery.' But I tell you that anyone who looks at a woman lustfully has already committed adultery with her in his heart" (Matthew 5:27-28).

Notes: Mark is tender at first, then sarcastic, and finally cruel. Susie is wounded throughout, but she is desperately lonely at the end. This sketch could be done with or without the TV in the background. Susie wants to confront Mark with what she has found. All Mark wants to do is take the dog for a walk.

1 **SETTING:** The kitchen. Susie is finishing some baking when Mark
2   enters.
3
4 **MARK:** *(Kissing her on the neck or tenderly touching her shoulder)*
5   **Hey, honey, have you seen the dog chain? I was gonna take**
6   **Alfie for a walk.**
7 **SUSIE:** *(Coldly, without looking up)* **No. It's probably in the**
8   **cupboard above the washing machine.**
9 **MARK:** *(Grabbing a cookie off the table)* **Hmmm. I looked there**
10   **already. I didn't see it.**
11 **SUSIE: Mark, I need to tell you something —**
12 **MARK:** *(Talking with his mouth full)* **What's that?**
13 **SUSIE: Could you sit down for a minute?**
14 **MARK: Naw, I gotta go walk the dog.**
15 **SUSIE: I really need to talk!**
16 **MARK: All right, hold on — is this gonna be one of those long**
17   **bonding talks like you always want to have after going on**
18   **those women's retreats?** *(To Off-stage)* **Hey, Alfie! It's gonna**
19   **be awhile. Just use the bathroom down the hall ... There you**
20   **go, boy! And don't forget to put the seat back down when**
21   **you're done!**
22 **SUSIE:** *(Hurt)* **Quit it!**
23 **MARK: Lighten up! I was just kidding around. What's the big**
24   **deal?**
25 **SUSIE: I'm trying to talk to you about something important!**
26 **MARK: Well, I'm trying to find the chain to take our dog for a**
27   **walk! I'm not really in the mood to** *(Sarcastically)*
28   **"communicate my feelings"! Now, I looked in the cupboard,**
29   **so if the chain is in there, it's invisible.** *(Grabbing another*
30   *cookie, miming his search)*
31 **SUSIE:** *(Partly under her breath, accusingly)* **Not all chains are**
32   **visible.**
33 **MARK:** *(Stopping mid-chew)* **What's that supposed to mean?**
34 **SUSIE: It just means, well, that sometimes people get controlled by**
35   **something, and they don't even realize it.**

1   MARK: *(Overly melodramatic)* **OK, all right. You have my**
2   **attention. What are you trying to say?**

3   SUSIE: I was downloading some recipes off the Internet, and while
4   I was searching, I came across some of the sites you've been
5   visiting.

6   MARK: What sites?

7   SUSIE: I think you know.

8   MARK: Look, I don't have time for this.

9   SUSIE: I saw the files you downloaded. You told me you wouldn't
10 look at that stuff anymore.

11 MARK: So you were spying on me.

12 SUSIE: No, I wasn't spying on you. Stop blaming me. I saw the
13 pictures, Mark. And it hurt.

14 MARK: Looking at a few pictures doesn't hurt anyone.

15 SUSIE: It hurts me!

16 MARK: Why should it hurt you?

17 SUSIE: Because I can't measure up to 'em! Is that what you're
18 thinking about when we're alone together?

19 MARK: Look, Susie. You're getting all carried away here.

20 SUSIE: And it changes you! You treat me differently.

21 MARK: *(Shocked)* What are you talking about? No, I don't.

22 SUSIE: We're not close like we used to be. You're less patient. You
23 get angry so quickly. You're not satisfied with me. That's what
24 hurts the most.

25 MARK: What do you want from me? It's just a few pictures! It's
26 not like I went out and had an affair or anything! I'm not
27 sleeping with anyone else!

28 SUSIE: You're not sleeping with me.

29 MARK: What?!

30 SUSIE: You're sleeping with them.

31 MARK: Who?

32 SUSIE: The girls in those pictures.

33 MARK: This is ridiculous. What about you?

34 SUSIE: What about me?

35 MARK: Who else are you sleeping with?

1   SUSIE: No one!
2   MARK: Oh, yeah? What about your soap operas? Every afternoon
3   for two hours, you sit watching that trash! And how about all
4   those cheap romance novels you're always reading? Yeah, I've
5   paged through them. They don't have pictures, but they sure
6   have descriptions.
7   SUSIE: Those things are different!
8   MARK: *(Sensing a chance to win the argument)* No they're not!
9   You're thinking about other men!
10 SUSIE: You're just trying to change the subject.
11 MARK: Oh, really? Invisible chains ... Being controlled by
12   something and not realizing it ... Sounds like the same subject
13   to me.
14 SUSIE: I don't want to talk about this anymore.
15 MARK: You're the one who brought it up! *(Pounding the table)* You
16   want to talk, let's talk!
17 SUSIE: Stop it! *(Starting to cry)* Please stop. You're scaring me.
18 MARK: *(Cruelly sarcastic)* Yeah, well, I wouldn't want to do that,
19   would I? I'm taking the dog outside — with a chain or
20   without one. We can talk later. *(He begins to exit and calls back
21   over his shoulder.)* Enjoy your soaps.
22 SUSIE: *(To herself)* But I want to enjoy you ... I want to enjoy you
23   ... *(Tries to start baking again, but she can't stop crying. Finally
24   she turns off the TV, puts her hands up to her face, and freezes.
25   Blackout.)*
26
27
28
29
30
31
32
33
34
35

Prodigal

Summary: Andrea ran away two years ago. Her father still waits for her return.

Purpose: To portray the longing of a parent for a child in trouble.

Time: 4-6 minutes

Tone: Serious

Cast: Andrea — A teenage runaway longing for home (female); James — Her loving father (male)

Costume: Old, dirty clothes for Andrea

Props/Set: Girl's bedroom scene with a bed, stuffed animals, dresser, mirror, a music box that plays a lullaby; a park bench

Themes: Choices, faith, family life, forgiveness, grace, guilt, hiding, home, hope, life, love, new life, parenting, questions, repentance, running away, second chances, teenagers

Text: "We had to celebrate and be glad, because this brother of yours was dead and is alive again: he was lost and is found" (Luke 15:32).

Notes: On one side of the stage, set up the bedroom scene. On the other side of the stage is a park bench. Andrea is dressed in old, dirty clothes. Andrea and James never make eye contact with each other. Each freezes when the other person is delivering his or her lines.

1   *SETTING:* Andrea is on a park bench in the middle of the city. James
2   is in her old bedroom back home.
3
4   **ANDREA:** *(Seated on the park bench)* **The day I left home, I didn't**
5   **look back. I had no desire to. Not then. Not ever.**
6   **JAMES:** *(Seated on the bed)* **The day she walked out the door, I**
7   **couldn't stop crying. I knew what the world was like out there**
8   **beyond the fence.**
9   **ANDREA: I was happy to finally be free! Free to be myself! Free**
10   **to chase my dreams and live my own life for a change!**
11 **JAMES: I wanted to stop her, but I knew her mind was made up.**
12   **If she didn't want to be here, I couldn't make her stay. It had**
13   **to be her decision.**
14 **ANDREA:** *(Standing up)* **At first it was fun! No one telling me what**
15   **to do anymore! Parties every night! Clubs to go to! Concerts**
16   **to attend! Everything was real and bigger than life! It was**
17   **great! For a while. But then, slowly, things began to change.**
18 **JAMES: Of course I looked for her. I went to the city every day. I**
19   **checked the bars. The street corners. The hospitals. Even the**
20   **morgues. Nothing.**
21 **ANDREA: I didn't have a place to stay, so I moved in with some**
22   **friends. The parties started lasting longer and longer until we**
23   **hardly ever left the apartment.**
24 **JAMES: For two years, nothing.**
25 **ANDREA: It's kind of a blur. People came and left. They laughed**
26   **with me and held me and slept with me ... and then they left.**
27   **They all left. I was so lonely. I started to cry into my pillow**
28   **when I woke up ... alone. But no one was there to hear me.**
29 **JAMES:** *(Gesturing to the dresser)* **I kept her room just the way it**
30   **was when she left.** *(Picking up the music box)* **I gave this to her**
31   **when she was four ...**
32 **ANDREA: Finally all my money was gone. My friends didn't want**
33   **me hanging around living off them, so I had to sell the only**
34   **thing I had left. Myself.**
35 **JAMES: She used to say, "Daddy, it sounds like angels singing! Is**

1	that what the angels sing?" And I nodded and smiled. It was
2	the angel's song. It was our song.
3	ANDREA: Every night I just wished one of the men would say, "I
4	love you." Even if he didn't mean it. I just wanted to hear
5	those words. Daddy used to say them to me every night when
6	he tucked me in bed. "Goodnight, princess! I love you." He
7	called me his little princess.
8	JAMES: Sometimes I like to come in here and look in her mirror
9	and imagine that it's her staring back at me instead of just a
10	reflection of myself. But it isn't her at all. She's gone.
11	ANDREA: I walked past a store window yesterday and saw my
12	reflection. People used to tell me all the time that I looked like
13	Dad. "What a resemblance!" they'd say. "Eyes just like your
14	father's." Not anymore. My eyes are too tired. And hollow.
15	I'm all worn out and used up — like a piece of trash.
16	JAMES: She's my only daughter. She's everything to me. My
17	precious little princess. I'd give anything to see her again.
18	She's priceless.
19	ANDREA: I'm worthless. I'm a failure. I'm nothing anymore. Last
20	week I thought about calling home. I really did. But I'm sure
21	Dad wouldn't want to talk to me. *(From here, the conversation*
22	*is a little quicker. They're almost interrupting each other. Since*
23	*their lines alternate so quickly, each should scan the audience —*
24	*not freeze — while the other speaks.)*
25	JAMES: I just wish she'd call.
26	ANDREA: After what I've done …
27	JAMES: I don't care what she's done …
28	ANDREA: After what I've become …
29	JAMES: Every day I stare out the window …
30	ANDREA: Sometimes I feel like one of those little girls in the fairy
31	tales, lost in the woods.
32	JAMES: … Waiting. Hoping …
33	ANDREA: … Stumbling in the dark, looking for breadcrumbs,
34	JAMES: … For the day when my little princess …
35	ANDREA: … Trying to find my way …

1   **JAMES:** ... **Will come ...**
2   **ANDREA:** ... **Back ...**
3   **TOGETHER:** ... **Home.** *(JAMES winds up the music box and as it*
4   *plays, he exits off the other side of the stage from ANDREA. She*
5   *hums the tune. Slowly the music and the lights fade out until we*
6   *only hear her humming. Then that, too, fades away.)*
7
8
9
10
11
12
13
14
15
16
17
18
19
20
21
22
23
24
25
26
27
28
29
30
31
32
33
34
35

Hide and Seek

Summary: Kali and her brother Todd have returned to their old house to pack up their father's things so he can move in with Todd and his family. As they reminisce, some difficult memories come to the surface.

Purpose: To show that we need to be there for people who've experienced tragedy.

Time: 6-8 minutes

Tone: Serious

Cast: Kali — A twentysomething lady who was abused as a child (female); Todd — Her older brother who didn't know about it (male)

Props/Set: Glasses of lemonade, photo album, papers, chair, couch, coffee table

Themes: Abuse, choices, compassion, family life, hiding, home, listening, love, questions, regrets, relationships, second chances, secrets

Text: "Praise be to the God and Father of our Lord Jesus Christ, the Father of compassion and the God of all comfort, who comforts us in all our troubles, so that we can comfort those in any trouble with the comfort we ourselves have received from God" (2 Corinthians 1:3-4).

Notes: Since this sketch approaches the topic of child abuse, it's packed with emotional intensity. As you direct it, remember that Kali has never shared this information with anyone else. Todd isn't the villain; he just never noticed what was happening to Kali.

1   *SETTING:* The living room of the house Kali and Todd grew up in. As
2   the scene opens, they are seated on the couch going through a pile
3   of legal papers. A photo album and glasses of lemonade are on the
4   table.
5

6   TODD: *(Sighing)* I guess I never thought it would happen like this.
7   KALI: Me neither. I mean, Dad was so healthy. And then all of a
8   sudden ...
9   TODD: Yeah. It's gonna be kind of weird having him live with
10   Carol and me. But I think the kids are really gonna like
11   having Grandpa around.
12 KALI: Well, he'll like being near his grandkids, that much is for
13   sure.
14 TODD: Yeah.
15 KALI: *(Gesturing)* Todd, are you sure all this stuff is gonna fit in
16   your house?
17 TODD: Yeah, I think so. He's gonna be staying in the basement so
18   he doesn't have to go up and down the stairs. There's a
19   bathroom and a bedroom down there, and we fixed up the
20   garage as a little living room. All we did was store junk in
21   there anyway.
22 KALI: *(Looking around)* And we're actually gonna sell this old
23   place.
24 TODD: Yup. It was a good house to grow up in, though. Lots of
25   room in the back yard, that park nearby. We could walk to
26   school. Not a lot of traffic ... Remember how we always used
27   to play games at night, you know, running around the
28   neighborhood?
29 KALI: Capture the flag!
30 TODD: Yeah! And kick the can.
31 KALI: And hide and seek.
32 TODD: Yeah! I used to love playing hide and seek.
33 KALI: I always used to hide behind that big tree in the back yard.
34 TODD: *(Smiling)* I know! I always found you there in the exact
35   same place!

1   KALI: *(Warmly)* **Well, you were older! You were supposed to take it**
2   **easy on your little sister!**
3   TODD: **Take it easy? On you?!**
4   KALI: **Yeah! Make sure I'd win once in a while.**
5   TODD: **The way I remember it, you didn't need any help winning.**
6   **You were always beating the boys at everything. It was like**
7   **your mission!**
8   KALI: **Let's hear it for girl power!**
9   TODD: **Remember that time we were playing when Uncle Amos**
10   **came over?**
11   KALI: *(Looking down)* **No ... I don't think so ...**
12   TODD: **Oh, c'mon, you know. It was summer and we'd all been**
13   **swimming that afternoon, and we decided to play hide and**
14   **seek just as it started to get dark. I think Uncle Amos was**
15   **bringing some parts from his shop for Dad's car or something.**
16   **You remember, right?**
17   KALI: *(Paging through a photo album on the coffee table)* **I don't**
18   **know ...**
19   TODD: **It was that time you hid in the closet down in the basement!**
20   **Remember? I couldn't find you 'cause you went to a new**
21   **place. Then, right after you hid, he came over and everyone**
22   **got to talking, and no one came looking for you. I thought**
23   **you'd remember that.**
24   KALI: **No —**
25   TODD: *(Shrugging it off)* **Hmmm. OK, whatever ...** *(Paging through*
26   *the album on his own)* **Oh, look at this! Remember when we**
27   **went to Disney World when you were twelve? Back when**
28   **Mom was still alive?**
29   KALI: *(To herself, remembering)* **The game ended and all the other**
30   **kids went home and forgot about me ...**
31   TODD: **I loved Magic Kingdom. Now it's so expensive that I doubt**
32   **I'll ever be able to take my own kids —**
33   KALI: **I tried to get out, but the door was jammed —**
34   TODD: **The trip home took forever! I think we must have stopped**
35   **at every campground from Orlando to here —**

1   KALI: It was fun for a while, you know, hiding. But only as long as
2   I thought you guys were looking for me. When I realized no
3   one was coming for me, I got really scared. I started crying.
4   TODD: *(Finally listening)* Yeah! That's it! See? You do remember!
5   We heard you screaming and found you in the closet. You
6   were pretty freaked out.
7   KALI: I'd been in there for nearly an hour ...
8   TODD: Wow. Yeah, that musta been scary. *(Gathering the papers)*
9   So, anyway — let's get this stuff cleared out of here so the real
10   estate guy can start showing people the house.
11   KALI: There's no loneliness like the loneliness you feel when
12   you're hiding and no one is looking for you ...
13   TODD: *(Overwhelmed)* Whew. This is going be a mess sorting
14   through all these papers ...
15   KALI: *(Remembering)* He touched me.
16   TODD: Huh?
17   KALI: Uncle Amos. He touched me.
18   TODD: What are you talking about?
19   KALI: Whenever he came over. Whenever he visited. He'd always
20   find an excuse to be alone with me —
21   TODD: Kali, are you saying what I think you're saying?
22   KALI: That's why I started hiding in the closet. So maybe he
23   wouldn't find me. But he always found me ...
24   TODD: *(Shocked)* Uncle Amos?
25   KALI: He said it'd be our little secret. That I was special. That he
26   loved me ...
27   TODD: *(Realizing what she means)* You've never told anyone
28   before ... Kali! Why didn't you tell us?!
29   KALI: I was scared no one would believe me. You know how close
30   Amos and Dad were. And he said he'd kill my cat if I ever
31   told ...
32   TODD: Oh, Kali! I don't know what to say. I had no idea!
33   KALI: Were you looking for me?
34   TODD: Huh?
35   KALI: Looking for your little sister. Didn't you ever wonder why

1   he came over so often?

2   TODD: No. I never thought about it.

3   KALI: I kept thinking, "Todd will notice. Dad will find out. Then

4   it'll stop." I kept hoping you or Dad would walk in on us. I

5   wanted to escape, but I didn't know how. After a while, I felt

6   like no one was looking for me. So then I found other ways to

7   hide ...

8   TODD: I'm so sorry. I wish I would have known! I wish I could

9   have stopped it.

10   KALI: *(Starting to cry)* I don't blame you, Todd, I just wanted it to

11   stop. I didn't think anyone would believe me.

12   TODD: Oh, Kali, I believe you.

13   KALI: *(Crying now)* You do?

14   TODD: Yeah. And it's not your fault.

15   KALI: I didn't know how to make him stop —

16   TODD: Listen to me, it's not your fault. It's not. It's his fault.

17   KALI: *(Crying)* I've been waiting a long time to hear someone say

18   that.

19   TODD: C'mere, Kali. *(KALI leans over the couch to bury her head in*

20   *his shoulder.)*

21   KALI: It was so lonely.

22   TODD: You're not alone, sis. Not anymore ... *(Freeze. Fadeout.)*

23

24

25

26

27

28

29

30

31

32

33

34

35

The Men Next Door

Summary: When two men move into the house next to Linda, she starts spreading rumors about them until Karyn offers alternate possibilities to Linda's assumptions.

Purpose: To convict people of judging others based solely on appearances.

Time: 6-8 minutes

Tone: Lighthearted, but with a serious undertone

Cast: Linda — A busybody who thinks her new neighbors are gay (female); Karyn — Her friend who is tired of Linda's gossiping (female)

Props/Set: Two shopping carts, various food items; shelves stocked with food (if desired)

Themes: Assumptions, church issues, gossip, homosexuality, judging, love, modern life, stereotypes

Text: "Brothers, do not slander one another. Anyone who speaks against his brother or judges him speaks against the law and judges it. When you judge the law, you are not keeping it, but sitting in judgment on it. There is only one Lawgiver and Judge, the one who is able to save and destroy. But you — who are you to judge your neighbor?" (James 4:11-12).

Notes: This sketch brings up the sensitive and sometimes difficult topic of homosexuality in a humorous and honest way. Believers are not called to judge others but to love and accept them, even when they don't agree with their lifestyles.

1   ***SETTING:*** The aisle of a grocery store. As the scene opens, Linda and
2   Karyn are each pushing a shopping cart when they run into each
3   other in the center aisle of the store. They start talking about
4   things in the neighborhood.
5
6   **LINDA: Karyn?**
7   **KARYN: Oh, Linda!**
8   **LINDA: Hey! How are you?**
9   **KARYN: I'm great!** *(Picking up a giant bag of chips from her cart)*
10   **Just picking up a few things for the boys. You know how they**
11   **go through their food.**
12   **LINDA: Yeah ... Tim and I are having a barbeque tonight, and I**
13   **forgot I didn't have any barbeque sauce or meat.**
14   **KARYN: Can't have a barbeque without meat, can you?**
15   **LINDA: No ...** *(Leaning close and lowering her voice)* **Say, did you**
16   **hear about the people who moved in next door to us?**
17   **KARYN: No. You mean someone finally bought that old place?**
18   **LINDA:** *(Judgmentally)* **Yeah. Two men: Jack and Leroy.**
19   **KARYN: Oh.**
20   **LINDA:** *(Suggestively)* **Two men.**
21   **KARYN: Yeah, you said that.**
22   **LINDA: And no women ...**
23   **KARYN: Uh-huh.**
24   **LINDA: Just two men and no women.**
25   **KARYN:** *(Not getting the significance)* **OK. And?**
26   **LINDA: Don't you get it? They're ... um ...** *(Looking from side to*
27   *side)* **you know ...**
28   **KARYN: Your new neighbors?**
29   **LINDA: No! They're ... partners.**
30   **KARYN: Oh, yeah? What kinda business are they in?**
31   **LINDA: They're not in business together ... they're the other kind**
32   **of partners.**
33   **KARYN:** *(The exchange is quick.)* **Oh.**
34   **LINDA: Uh-huh!**
35   **KARYN: Hmmm.**

1   LINDA: Yeah.

2   KARYN: Huh.

3   LINDA: Right.

4   KARYN: Well.

5   LINDA: Can you believe it?

6   KARYN: Well, are you sure?

7   LINDA: Well ... Janice saw them moving in and told me she
8   recognized Jack from a meeting they had for Little League.
9   He coached a team her son played against last year, and the
10   kids were always talking about how he had, you know, come
11   out.

12 KARYN: So you're not sure?

13 LINDA: Why else would they be living together?

14 KARYN: I don't know. Could they be friends maybe? Or
15   brothers? Do you know they're not brothers?

16 LINDA: Not for sure ... But two men don't buy a house together
17   unless they're ... partners.

18 KARYN: You don't know that!

19 LINDA: They're gay! There, I said it. Jack and Leroy are gay. I
20   have two gay men living next door to me! In this town! Can
21   you believe it?

22 KARYN: *(Acting as if it's terrible news)* What should we do?

23 LINDA: I don't know! That's what I wanted to talk to you about.

24 KARYN: *(Mocking LINDA)* Maybe we should contact the mayor
25   and see if he can issue an ordinance against men staying in the
26   same house, or we could picket the neighborhood long enough
27   and maybe they'll move away —

28 LINDA: Do you think that would work?

29 KARYN: I was kidding!

30 LINDA: Oh. You're not taking this very seriously, are you? Don't
31   you find it upsetting that they're living an *unbiblical* lifestyle?

32 KARYN: Not really. First of all, you don't even know if they're gay
33   or not! And second, I think you're blowing this whole thing
34   out of proportion.

35 LINDA: Don't you know what the *Bible* says about —

1   **KARYN: I know what the Bible says.**

2   **LINDA: Well!** *(As if that settles everything)* **What would I say if Jack**

3   **or Leroy came walking up to me?**

4   **KARYN: How about, "Hi! Welcome to the neighborhood!"**

5   **LINDA:** *(Disgusted)* **You're not being very helpful.**

6   **KARYN: Well, you're not being very rational. So two men moved**

7   **in next door. Big deal! You don't know anything about them!**

8   **For example, are they nice?**

9   **LINDA: I don't know.**

10   **KARYN: Do they go to church?**

11   **LINDA: I doubt it!**

12   **KARYN: Have you even met them?**

13   **LINDA: I'm not sure I want to!**

14   **KARYN: Is either of them a Christian?**

15   **LINDA: How could they be Christian men and gay at the same**

16   **time?!**

17   **KARYN: C'mon, name one Christian who doesn't have at least one**

18   **weakness in her life.**

19   **LINDA:** *(Overreacting)* **We're not talking about weaknesses here!**

20   **KARYN: Well, maybe we should be ... Listen — doesn't everybody**

21   **have certain weaknesses?**

22   **LINDA: Well, yeah.**

23   **KARYN: OK then ... What's your weakness?**

24   **LINDA: Mine?**

25   **KARYN: Yeah, you just agreed that everybody has one. What's**

26   **yours?**

27   **LINDA: Well, I don't know. I mean, I never thought about it, I**

28   **guess.**

29   **KARYN: I can give you a few ideas if you'd like ... if you're**

30   **interested.**

31   **LINDA:** *(Shocked)* **You're going to tell me what my weaknesses are?**

32   **KARYN: Sure, who better to? I'm your friend, aren't I?**

33   **LINDA:** *(Tentatively)* **Yeah. OK. Go ahead.**

34   **KARYN:** *(Rattling these off)* **How about being quick to judge,**

35   **talking about people behind their backs, looking down on**

1   others, thinking you're better than they are, spreading
2   slanderous rumors, gossiping —
3 LINDA: OK, OK. That's enough.
4 KARYN: Are you sure? I could keep going if you like.
5 LINDA: No, that's plenty.
6 KARYN: No more gossiping about Jack and Leroy, then?
7 LINDA: No more gossiping.
8 KARYN: And that includes bringing them up at church to pray for
9   them?
10 LINDA: You don't want me to pray for them?!
11 KARYN: Of course you can pray for them! Just don't use that as
12   an excuse to talk about them behind their backs! And first get
13   to know them and find out what kind of prayers they actually
14   need!
15 LINDA: OK.
16 KARYN: So you're gonna go visit them and welcome them to the
17   neighborhood?
18 LINDA: I couldn't do that!
19 KARYN: Why not? You need to get to know them, don't you?
20 LINDA: What if someone sees me talking to them?
21 KARYN: Maybe they'll think you finally got over your hang-ups
22   with people who are different from you.
23 LINDA: *(Hesitating)* OK. I'll think about it.
24 KARYN: Good.
25 LINDA: *(Whispering)* But what if I find out they're really gay?
26   Then what?
27 KARYN: What if they find out you're really a gossiper?
28 LINDA: I'm serious.
29 KARYN: Me, too. Love 'em. Care about 'em. That's what
30   "unconditional love" is all about. You don't love someone
31   because he acts a certain way. That's not love! If you really
32   love someone, you keep caring about him even though he
33   doesn't always measure up to your standards.
34 LINDA: *(Sighing)* Did anyone ever tell you you're annoying when
35   you're logical? *(KARYN smiles.)* All right. Well, I hope you got

1   enough food to fill up those boys of yours.
2   **KARYN: Probably not. Hey, have a good barbeque tonight.**
3   **LINDA: I will. And thanks.**
4   **KARYN: For what?**
5   **LINDA: For giving me something to chew on until then.** *(Freeze.*
6   *Fadeout.)*
7
8
9
10
11
12
13
14
15
16
17
18
19
20
21
22
23
24
25
26
27
28
29
30
31
32
33
34
35

Mirror, Mirror on the Wall

Summary: Renee is ready to face the world again after her unsuccessful suicide attempt. Joel is trying to support and encourage her.

Purpose: To show that none of us is perfect, regardless of appearance.

Time: 4-6 minutes

Tone: Serious

Cast: Renee — A still-unsure survivor of a suicide attempt (female); Joel — Her concerned husband (male)

Costumes: Joel is in a suit or nice outfit. Renee is wearing a nice dress with long sleeves.

Props/Set: Vanity mirror, a roll of gauze bandages, purse, makeup supplies.

Themes: Appearances, assumptions, authenticity, choices, coping, hiding, love, married life, questions, second chances, secrets, suicide

Text: "Let the morning bring me word of your unfailing love, for I have put my trust in you. Show me the way I should go, for to you I lift up my soul" (Psalm 143:8).

Notes: Before the sketch begins, wrap the gauze bandages around Renee's wrists. Be sure that her sleeves cover them so the audience doesn't see her wrists until Joel pulls back her sleeves.

1   ***SETTING:*** Renee and Joel's bedroom. She is wearing a loose-fitting
2   blouse or shirt that reaches past her wrists so no one in the
3   audience can see the bandages. As the scene opens, she is seated
4   in front of a vanity mirror, putting on her earrings and makeup.
5

6   **RENEE:** *(After a few moments of putting on her makeup, she begins to*
7   *look at her face from different angles in the mirror. Finally she*
8   *takes a deep breath and begins talking to herself.)* **Mirror, mirror**
9   **on the wall, who used to be the fairest of them all?** *(Posing as*
10   *a cheerleader)* **Cheerleader ...** *(Placing an imaginary crown on*
11   *her head)* **Homecoming court ...** *(Posing as a model)* **Even**
12   **modeling for two magazines ... Twenty pounds and two kids**
13   **and fifteen years ago ... I wonder what you'd say if you could**
14   **talk. "It's not that bad," or "You carry the weight very well,"**
15   **or "Time has been good to you ..."** No, you wouldn't
16   **sugarcoat anything. You'd be honest. You're always honest.**
17   *(Leaning close)* **I wonder what you'd say ...**
18   **JOEL:** *(From Off-stage)* **Hey, Honey? Almost ready for our big**
19   **date?**
20   **RENEE:** *(She is startled. It's almost like the mirror was speaking to*
21   *her. Responding to the Off-stage voice)* **Almost!** *(To her mirror)*
22   **For a minute there, I thought that was you! Just Joel. So ...**
23   **You tell it like it is, don't you? Zit on the chin. Nose too big.**
24   **Dark circles under the eyes. At least you tell me the truth, even**
25   **when it's ugly. There's something to that. Most people wouldn't**
26   **dare tell the truth ... I wouldn't dare tell the truth ... You see**
27   **me without my makeup. You accept me as is. That's nice. It's**
28   **just so hard smiling all the time ... So many roles ...** *(Quickly)*
29   **Playing the perfect wife and the caring mother and the**
30   **friendly neighbor. Commitments and expectations. At the**
31   **club. And the banquets. And the office. And church. Day in.**
32   **Day out. Week in. Week out. Always smiling ...** *(Pausing)* **And**
33   **now everyone will know ... How come it had to come to this?**
34   **Why couldn't I just stay beautiful?** *(Leaning toward the mirror)*
35   **Why do you have to be so honest?**

1   **JOEL:** *(Entering, straightening his tie)* **Dear, are you coming?**

2   **RENEE: Yeah.**

3   **JOEL:** *(Walking up to her)* **You OK?**

4   **RENEE: Yeah.**

5   **JOEL: You sure? I thought I heard you talking to someone.**

6   **RENEE:** *(Faking a smile at him)* **I'm good. So, what did you have in**
7   **mind for tonight?**

8   **JOEL: There's this new Bruce Willis** *(Or another popular actor)*
9   **movie I was hoping we could catch. It's kind of an action /**
10   **romance / adventure / comedy / thriller-thing. Looks good. By**
11   **the way ... how'd it go at the doctor's office this morning?**

12 **RENEE:** *(Looking back toward the mirror)* **It went well.**

13 **JOEL: Everything's all right?**

14 **RENEE: Yeah.**

15 **JOEL: So how does the movie sound?**

16 **RENEE: Well ... OK.**

17 **JOEL:** *(Putting his hands on her head and closing his eyes)* **Hmmm.**
18 **Joel the Magnificent senses that you would rather not go to**
19 **the movie ... Yes ... I'm getting an image here ...** *(Opening his*
20 *eyes and looking at her face in the mirror)* **Let me guess ...**
21 **You'd rather go for a walk down by the pier. Maybe get some**
22 **dessert. Talk. Bond. Stuff like that.**

23 **RENEE:** *(Smiling, amused)* **How do you do that?**

24 **JOEL: I'm a mind-reader ... Seriously, Renee, you can be honest**
25 **with me. You don't always have to try so hard to tell me what**
26 **you think I want to hear.**

27 **RENEE:** *(Looking down)* **I know.**

28 **JOEL: I mean it. I'll listen.**

29 **RENEE: It's hard sometimes. I just want you to be happy.**

30 **JOEL: Then let me in. Don't hide from me. I'd love to go for a**
31 **walk. I'll just rent the movie sometime. It'll be nice to talk ...**
32 **Renee ...**

33 **RENEE: I'm OK. Really.**

34 **JOEL:** *(Sound of a doorbell ringing Off-stage)* **OK. That's the baby**
35 **sitter. I'll go let her in.** *(Tenderly)* **By the way, you look great in**

1   that dress ...

2   **RENEE:** *(Smiling at him)* **Thanks.** *(To mirror after he leaves)* **He's**

3   **trying, isn't he? I know he is. I don't blame him. It's just so**

4   **hard ...** *(Finishing up her makeup)* **Well, here we go. Back to**

5   **the world ... See how much it's changed in the last couple**

6   **weeks.** *(Getting up)* **Mirror, mirror on the wall, who's the**

7   **fairest of them all?**

8   **JOEL:** *(Poking his head back into the room)* **Ready?**

9   **RENEE: Yeah. I'm putting my shoes on.**

10   **JOEL: You sure you're ready for this?**

11   **RENEE: Yeah.**

12   **JOEL: How are your wrists?**

13   **RENEE: Pretty good. Still sore.** *(JOEL slowly and tenderly pulls back*

14   *the sleeves of her shirt, revealing the bandages, then holding them*

15   *up to the audience)*

16   **JOEL: It takes a while to heal, doesn't it?**

17   **RENEE: Yeah, it can take a while ... The doctor said there'll be**

18   **scars ...**

19   **JOEL: We all have scars, Renee. It's part of being human. Some**

20   **are just easier to see than others —**

21   **RENEE: Or easier to hide.**

22   **JOEL: You don't need to hide them.**

23   **RENEE: The longer you live, the more scars you have.**

24   **JOEL:** *(Looking her in the eye, with feeling)* **The longer you live, the**

25   **longer you live ...** *(He rolls the sleeves back down, takes her*

26   *hand, and continues)* **with wrinkles and gray hair and stretch**

27   **marks and scars and all ... and it's OK. C'mon, let's go for a**

28   **walk.**

29   **RENEE:** *(As they turn to exit, she reaches out and touches her image*

30   *in the mirror, letting her fingers trail along her face. Then she*

31   *echoes his thought with feeling and with hope.)* **The longer you**

32   **live, the longer you live ...** *(As they exit, fadeout.)*

33

34

35

Secrets

Summary: When Ariel brings up her uncertainty about college and shares her dilemma, Jeanne finally reveals a secret of her own.

Purpose: To show the significance and value of each individual life.

Time: 6-8 minutes

Tone: Serious with lighthearted moments

Cast: Ariel — A pregnant teenager facing a tough choice (female); Jeanne — Her mother, who has a secret of her own (female)

Props/Set: College clothes, other student paraphernalia, car keys

Themes: Abortion, choices, family life, forgiveness, life, meaning, parenting, purpose, questions, role models, secrets, teenagers, trust

Text: "Likewise, teach the older women to be reverent in the way they live, not to be slanderers or addicted to much wine, but to teach what is good. Then they can train the younger women to love their husbands and children, to be self-controlled and pure" (Titus 2:3-5a).

Notes: The Christian community needs to continue emphasizing the value and significance of life and be there to support and help the women who choose it. This sketch explores those two responses. Ariel thinks she wants to have an abortion. Jeanne, her mother, is getting sentimental and doesn't realize Ariel's true dilemma.

1   *SETTING:* The driveway. As the scene opens, Ariel and Jeanne are
2   getting ready to say good-bye.
3
4   **JEANNE: Do you have your alarm clock?**
5   **ARIEL: Yeah.**
6   **JEANNE: What about your cell phone? Is it packed where you can**
7   **get to it?**
8   **ARIEL: I've got it, Mom!**
9   **JEANNE: And your class schedule and all those registration papers?**
10   **ARIEL: Mom, I've got them!**
11   **JEANNE: OK. I'm just trying to help. Don't get angry. Relax.**
12   **ARIEL: I *am* relaxed! You're the one who's tense!**
13   **JEANNE: Oh.**
14   **ARIEL: C'mon, Mom. Settle down. I'm only going off to college.**
15   **JEANNE:** *(Nostalgically)* **College. I can't believe you're really going**
16   **off to college.**
17   **ARIEL:** *(Holding up the car keys)* **Believe it. Here I go.**
18   **JEANNE:** *(Looking at her watch)* **I'm sorry I can't drive you myself,**
19   **but you know I couldn't get off work.**
20   **ARIEL:** *(Grabbing a bag of stuff)* **I know.**
21   **JEANNE: Off to school again ... I remember the day I stood by**
22   **that curb in Atlanta and watched you get on the bus when you**
23   **were five.**
24   **ARIEL:** *(Sighing)* **My first day of kindergarten, huh?**
25   **JEANNE:** *(Reenacting this as she tells it, nostalgically)* **Yeah. You**
26   **were carrying that cute little Minnie Mouse backpack. You**
27   **put one foot on the step to the bus and then you paused for a**
28   **moment, and you turned back and looked at me. I was crying**
29   **and waving, and you waved your little hand and blew me a**
30   **kiss.** *(Sensitively)* **Oh ... and then you turned and stepped onto**
31   **the bus and before the doors could close ...** *(Pausing)* **you**
32   **threw up all over the bus driver.**
33   **ARIEL:** *(Embarrassed)* **Yeah, you told me all about that before.**
34   **JEANNE: I had to drive you to school myself for the first month ...**
35   **ARIEL: Gosh. I hope that doesn't happen this time.** *(After a pause)*

1   It's always been tough for us to be apart, hasn't it?

2   JEANNE: Yeah. I tell my friends how close we are, and they can't

3   believe it. I tell them how we've never kept anything from

4   each other, and they just shake their heads.

5   ARIEL: It's always been just the two of us, right Mom?

6   JEANNE: *(Smiling)* Just me and you. Facing the world together.

7   ARIEL: Mom, you did a good job raising me alone.

8   JEANNE: *(Touched)* You think so?

9   ARIEL: Yeah. *(Warmly)* Of course you didn't do everything right,

10   but overall, you did OK. You came to my gymnastics meets

11   and planned those cool birthday parties for me and did your

12   best to help me with algebra.

13   JEANNE: I was never good at math.

14   ARIEL: I know, but you tried. And you let me have all those

15   sleepovers, and you were even there for me on prom night

16   when that jerk Buck Werner stood me up. We talked until like

17   two a.m.

18   JEANNE: I remember.

19   ARIEL: *(Awkwardly)* Well.

20   JEANNE: Well. Good-bye.

21   ARIEL: Good-bye ... *(Turning to leave, pausing, and coming back)* Um,

22   Mom. One time you told me I could tell you anything, right?

23   JEANNE: Yeah.

24   ARIEL: Did you mean it?

25   JEANNE: Of course.

26   ARIEL: Then I need to tell you something.

27   JEANNE: What?

28   ARIEL: Um ... Something happened to me, and I haven't told

29   anyone. And I'm a little scared.

30   JEANNE: What is it?

31   ARIEL: Whew. Wow ... this is hard to say. Mom, I'm pregnant.

32   JEANNE: What?

33   ARIEL: I just found out a couple days ago.

34   JEANNE: *(Sitting down)* I don't know what to say! Who's the father?

35   ARIEL: It doesn't matter.

1   JEANNE: What do you mean? It's William, isn't it?

2   ARIEL: That's not the point ... The point is, I'm scheduled to have

3   it taken care of on Tuesday after I've moved in —

4   JEANNE: *(Seriously)* Ariel, you don't want to do that —

5   ARIEL: Here's the thing. I know there's no way I could go to

6   college and raise a baby. I gotta give up one or the other. And

7   I do want to go. I know how important my going to college has

8   always been to you.

9   JEANNE: College can wait.

10   ARIEL: It's always been your dream for me.

11   JEANNE: College isn't the right choice.

12   ARIEL: I just wanted someone to be with me when it happens —

13   JEANNE: Listen to me, Ariel. You can't do this!

14   ARIEL: *(Upset)* Mom! Stop it! I don't get you. What — you want me

15   to just stay here and raise a baby — alone, like you did? Not go

16   to college? Give all that up because of one little mistake?!

17   You're always talking about how we're there for each other!

18   And now you're not even listening to me! Why won't you

19   support me? It's my body! It's my choice! I knew I shouldn't

20   have said anything. *(Turning to leave)* Look, I gotta get going —

21   JEANNE: I faced the same choice.

22   ARIEL: What?!

23   JEANNE: Right after I got pregnant with you, that's when your

24   dad left. One day I just came home and he wasn't there. He

25   never came back. I think he was scared of the idea of having a

26   kid around. I was scared, too. I knew I couldn't raise a baby

27   on my own —

28   ARIEL: Mom, do you know what you're saying?

29   JEANNE: I was young. I was alone. And I was pregnant. That's not

30   a good combination. There was nobody there for me, so I

31   decided ... to ... abort you.

32   ARIEL: Mom!

33   JEANNE: I scheduled the appointment. I even showed up early.

34   But as I sat there waiting in the doctor's office, I started

35   paging through the magazines, and on every page I saw

1 another kid. You know, ads for detergent and cough medicine
2 and clothes. But for me, they were ads for kids. Drinking
3 lemonade. Spilling jelly on the rug. Running across the lawn.
4 Laughing. And I wondered what your laughter would sound
5 like. What it would feel like to clean up your messes and wipe
6 away your tears. I made a decision I've never regretted.
7 ARIEL: You decided to keep me.
8 JEANNE: Yeah. I got up and walked out of there. I gave up my
9 dream of going to college. I chose a new dream. A new
10 priority. You.
11 ARIEL: But Mom, you were gonna kill me!
12 JEANNE: Yeah, *(Reaching over and touching ARIEL's arm)* but I
13 didn't.
14 ARIEL: Whoa. I'm not sure what to say. It's not every day you find
15 out your mom was gonna kill you.
16 JEANNE: Terminate the pregnancy, that's what they call it. That's
17 how they put it.
18 ARIEL: Yeah, I know ... I don't know what to do. Staying home
19 from college ... maybe never going ... It seems like I'd be
20 giving up an awful lot having this baby.
21 JEANNE: Ariel, I never regretted my choice. Never. I mean, look
22 at you! I love you! It hasn't been easy — God knows it hasn't
23 been easy — but it's all been worth it. And now you're
24 carrying a baby! A life. A life full of birthday parties and
25 sleepovers and prom nights.
26 ARIEL: I'm scared, Mom.
27 JEANNE: I know.
28 ARIEL: What am I gonna do? I'm seventeen years old and I'm
29 pregnant and —
30 JEANNE: You're not alone. You're not alone. Remember — me
31 and you?
32 ARIEL: Me and you. Facing the world together ... Hug me, Mom.
33 I'm scared. I wanna do what's right, but I'm scared. *(They hug
34 and freeze. Fadeout.)*
35

Harsh Mercy

Summary: Aaron rushes to his father's hospital room. But when his father asks him to call a doctor who helps terminally ill patients commit suicide, Aaron has to make a choice between what he thinks is right and what his father wants.

Purpose: To help people see the validity of life rather than "mercy" killing.

Time: 4-6 minutes

Tone: Serious

Cast: Thomas — A middle-aged man who has just suffered a heart attack (male); Aaron — His son who has never measured up to Dad's expectations (male)

Props/Set: Hospital bed, magazine, food tray, menu, duffel bag, business card, end table, glass of water

Themes: Choices, death, euthanasia, family life, life, love, relationships, second chances, suffering

Text: "This day I call heaven and earth as witnesses against you that I have set before you life and death, blessings and curses. Now choose life, so that you and your children may live and that you may love the Lord your God, listen to his voice, and hold fast to him" (Deuteronomy 30:19-20a).

Notes: Use dim lighting and ambiance sounds (announcements, machine noises, etc.) to create the mood of being in a hospital. Their conversation is marked by awkwardness. Be especially conscious of the pauses and timing as they try to figure out what to say and awkwardly interrupt each other.

1   *SETTING:* The critical care unit at a hospital. As the scene opens,
2   Thomas is asleep in bed and Aaron is seated by his side, reading
3   a magazine. The duffel bag is on the floor. The business card is on
4   the nearby table.
5
6   AARON: *(Reading; finally, THOMAS stirs.)* **Dad? You awake?**
7   THOMAS: **Aaron? Is that you?**
8   AARON: **Yeah. I caught the earliest flight I could.**
9   THOMAS: **How long you been here?**
10   AARON: **Oh, I don't know. A couple hours, I guess. How are you**
11   **doing?**
12   THOMAS: **How do you expect me to be doing with these tubes in**
13   **my arms and doctors poking at me every half hour and nurses**
14   **sticking needles into my leg every time I wake up —**
15   AARON: **OK, sorry I asked … Here, um … you want something to**
16   **eat?**
17   THOMAS: **No. Their food is terrible. It tastes like the stuff we used**
18   **to eat in the army.**
19   AARON: *(Putting the tray back down)* **Right.**
20   THOMAS: **So how are you doing?**
21   AARON: **I'm good.**
22   THOMAS: **What about your job?**
23   AARON: **It's pretty good.**
24   THOMAS: *(Disappointed with his son)* **My son, the English teacher.**
25   **Coulda been a lawyer, made some money. But no, he had to be**
26   **a high school teacher.**
27   AARON: **I like teaching, Dad.**
28   THOMAS: **Huh. You still driving that Honda?**
29   AARON: **Yeah, Dad.**
30   THOMAS: **I hate foreign cars. Cost us American jobs is all they do.**
31   **You still fish?**
32   AARON: *(Sighing)* **Not too much, no.**
33   THOMAS: **I used to take you fishing every summer. You loved**
34   **to fish when you were a kid … And my granddaughter — how**
35   **is she?**

1   AARON: She's good. She stays with her mom, you know.

2   THOMAS: *(Cuttingly)* How long were you two married again?

3   AARON: Four years.

4   THOMAS: *(As THOMAS says these words, AARON mouths them. He's*
5   *heard all this before.)* Your mom and I were married forty-one
6   years. No one stays married that long anymore. Everyone's
7   getting divorced these days. Everyone. Even my own son.

8   AARON: *(Trying to change the subject)* Dad, do you want some
9   water or something?

10 THOMAS: I miss her.

11 AARON: Who?

12 THOMAS: Your mother.

13 AARON: Yeah, Dad. Me, too.

14 THOMAS: She used to make this homemade chicken noodle soup
15   when I was sick. Grew that celery herself in the garden. I
16   don't know what all she put in that thing, but it sure was good.
17   Always made me feel better.

18 AARON: I can see if they have some kind of soup on the menu here
19   ... *(Picking up a menu from the hospital)*

20 THOMAS: No. It wouldn't be the same ... Sometimes when I go to
21   sleep, I can still feel her rolling over next to me ... *(After a*
22   *longer pause)* Aaron, I've been doing a lot of thinking these last
23   couple days.

24 AARON: Yeah?

25 THOMAS: I don't have much time left.

26 AARON: Don't talk like that.

27 THOMAS: It's true. And I don't wanna live like this.

28 AARON: Live like what?

29 THOMAS: Like this! Tubes and doctors and tests! *(Turning to*
30   *AARON, grabbing his arm, and whispering urgently)* I want you
31   to do something for me.

32 AARON: What's that, Dad?

33 THOMAS: Help me out ... Hurry it along ...

34 AARON: What's that supposed to mean?

35 THOMAS: You know. Pull the plug.

1   AARON: Dad! I didn't fly all the way over here to listen to you talk
2   like that!
3   THOMAS: There's no one else.
4   AARON: Then there's no one at all. I am not gonna kill my own
5   father!
6   THOMAS: Remember when you were a kid and your dog got hit
7   by that pickup truck?
8   AARON: Yeah.
9   THOMAS: Remember how we took it to the vet, and he said we
10   should stop its suffering and put it out of its misery?
11   AARON: Dad —
12   THOMAS: I'm suffering, Aaron. And I'm not gonna get any better.
13   We both know that. I'm asking you to put me out of my
14   misery.
15   AARON: You're not a dog, you're a person! You're my dad!
16   THOMAS: *(After a pause)* Yeah, I thought you might say all that,
17   so I asked one of the nurses ... She left the card of a doctor
18   who specializes in these things. It's on the table over there. I
19   need you to call him for me. They're supposed to have a
20   family member's permission —
21   AARON: No!
22   THOMAS: All you gotta do is call him.
23   AARON: Do you even know what you're saying?
24   THOMAS: Yes, I do.
25   AARON: This is crazy, Dad. I'm not gonna do it!
26   THOMAS: *(Getting worked up)* You never could do anything right,
27   could you? Never would listen to your old man! *(Starts*
28   *coughing and wheezing.)* I miss your mother, don't you
29   understand? Can't you do one thing right?! *(Really wheezing*
30   *now)*
31   AARON: Dad, Dad, calm down. There, lie down on your side. Just
32   rest for a few minutes. *(THOMAS rolls over on his side, and*
33   *AARON places his hand on his father's shoulder. In a moment*
34   *THOMAS is breathing more deeply. He is resting.)* One thing,
35   huh? Can't I do one thing right? Yeah, I can. *(Rips up the*

1   *business card.)*
2   **THOMAS:** *(Mumbling)* **What did you say?**
3   **AARON: Nothing, Dad. Go to sleep. I'll be here when you wake up.**
4   **I promise.** *(Freeze. Fadeout.)*
5
6
7
8
9
10
11
12
13
14
15
16
17
18
19
20
21
22
23
24
25
26
27
28
29
30
31
32
33
34
35

Caught in the Current

Summary: Randy and Kiera met in college, fell in love and started their life together. But since they won't take the time to develop their relationship, things don't end up like they expected.

Purpose: To show how easy it is for couples to drift apart.

Time: 8-10 minutes

Tone: Serious with lighthearted moments

Cast: Randy — A normal American guy (male); Kiera — A normal American woman (female); Stagehand — To play taped sound effects

Costumes: Casual dress that can be altered slightly to show the passage of time. Specifics include sandals and a hair scrunchie for Kiera; and glasses, an oxford shirt, and a sweater for Randy.

Props/Set: Book backpacks, purse, reading glasses, briefcase, checkbook, two cell phones, a small piece of driftwood, box with a ring in it, textbooks, magazine, baby blanket, two mugs, two bowls and spoons, toaster and bread, pile of papers, two chairs

Themes: Ambition, choices, communication, consequences, distractions, divorce, excuses, family life, life, love, married life, modern life, parenting, priorities, promises, regrets

Text: "'I hate divorce,' says the Lord God of Israel, 'and I hate a man's covering himself with violence as well as with his garments,' says the Lord Almighty. So guard yourself in your spirit, and do not break faith" (Malachi 2:16).

Notes: Sound effects of the wind blowing and a baby crying are needed. When the time shifts, Randy and Kiera remain frozen On-stage. Then, as the transitional music fades, they step into the next scene of their lives.

1   ***SETTING:*** Each vignette is a different scene as we see this couple pass
2   through life. The action begins on a college campus, just outside
3   the library. Kiera is walking across the stage.
4
5   **RANDY:** *(With backpack slung over one shoulder, sweater tied around*
6   *his waist, catching up with KIERA)* **Hey.**
7   **KIERA:** *(Wearing sandals, carrying an armload of books, walking to*
8   *class)* **Hey.**
9   **RANDY:** *(Now they're walking together.)* **Aren't you in my**
10   **economics class?**
11   **KIERA: With Thomason? Yeah. I'm Kiera.**
12   **RANDY: Kiera, cool, that's pretty. I'm Randy.** *(They stop walking to*
13   *shake hands.)*
14   **KIERA: Hi, Randy.**
15   **RANDY: Hi, Kiera.**
16   **KIERA: So.**
17   **RANDY: So.**
18   **KIERA: So.**
19   **RANDY: Yeah. Well, it's good to meet you.**
20   **KIERA: You, too.**
21   **RANDY: OK then.**
22   **KIERA: OK.**
23   **RANDY: Um, maybe we could get together and study sometime —**
24   **you know, for economics.**
25   **KIERA: Sure. Yeah. That'd be nice.**
26   **RANDY: Really?**
27   **KIERA: Yeah.**
28   **RANDY: Good.**
29   **KIERA: Good.**
30   **RANDY: OK.**
31   **KIERA:** *(Sweetly, over her shoulder as she walks away)* **'Bye.**
32   **RANDY: 'Bye.** *(Watching her as she leaves. Then he makes a fist and*
33   *pumps his arm as if to say, "Yes!" She pauses on the other side of*
34   *the stage, looks up, smiles dreamily, sighs, and freezes. Transition*
35   *sound of wind blowing plays. In this scene, they're at the beach,*

1   *walking hand in hand. As the music fades, RANDY puts his bag*
2   *on the table; KIERA puts her books on the table, kicks off her*
3   *sandals and takes RANDY's hand. Then they step into the scene.)*
4 KIERA: Oh ... I love the ocean!
5 RANDY: Yeah, me, too.
6 KIERA: I like to feel the sand squish between my toes ... see the
7   sunset ... watch the driftwood floating along ... *(Pointing)* See
8   how it kinda gets caught in the current? It's like it doesn't
9   even notice it's going in a new direction. And slowly, one wave
10   at a time, it just drifts away ...
11 RANDY: Yeah, that's pretty cool.
12 KIERA: Oh, look! *(Picking up a piece of driftwood)* Here!
13 RANDY: Oh. Thanks.
14 KIERA: *(Suggestively)* So do you know what day it is today, Randy?
15 RANDY: I think it's Wednesday.
16 KIERA: No, I mean what day it is?
17 RANDY: You mean it's not Wednesday?
18 KIERA: Randy! It's our anniversary! Of the day we first met
19   outside the library. Remember? One year ago today.
20 RANDY: Oh, *that* day!
21 KIERA: Yeah. *(Leaning close to him)*
22 RANDY: So ...
23 KIERA: So ...
24 RANDY: How long do you think we'll be together?
25 KIERA: I don't know.
26 RANDY: How about ... *(Pulling out a box)* a lifetime?
27 KIERA: *(Flustered)* Randy?
28 RANDY: *(Kneeling)* Kiera Wallace, would you marry me?
29 KIERA: But I thought you wanted to wait until you were out of
30   college!
31 RANDY: Not anymore. I don't wanna wait. Let's get married now!
32   Next month! We can make it. We love each other, don't we?
33 KIERA: Yes. Yes we do. And yes I will! Yes! Yes! *(They freeze.*
34   *Transition sound of wind blowing. In this scene, they're back at*
35   *home, in the kitchen. RANDY slips off his sweater. He is reading*

1   *a pile of textbooks. To set the scene, he puts his glasses on. KIERA*
2   *slips her sandals back on, grabs her purse, and pulls her hair*
3   *back, like she is going to work.)*
4   **KIERA:** *(Searching)* **Have you seen my keys?** *(No answer from*
5   *RANDY.)* **Randy! Have you seen my keys?**
6   **RANDY:** *(Without looking up)* **No.**
7   **KIERA: I'm late for work.**
8   **RANDY:** *(Still not looking up)* **You can take mine. They're on the**
9   **counter over there.**
10   **KIERA: You could make eye contact with me once in a while ...**
11   **You used to like looking into my eyes.**
12   **RANDY:** *(Looking up and sighing)* **Look. We both thought it would**
13   **be a good idea for me to go on to graduate school, right?**
14   **Remember? M.B.A.? Job security? Management position?**
15   **It's just a lot of work right now.**
16   **KIERA: I know. But it's just that, well, I hardly ever see you**
17   **anymore. I'm working all the time, and you're always doing**
18   **your research. I miss you.**
19   **RANDY: When I finish my thesis, things'll slow down. I promise.**
20   **We can go on a little vacation or something, OK? Maybe back**
21   **to the beach again.**
22   **KIERA: OK. By the way, happy anniversary.**
23   **RANDY:** *(Looking back at his books)* **Oh, yeah. You, too.** *(They*
24   *freeze. Transition sound of wind blowing. In this scene, they're in*
25   *the living room. It's late at night, and RANDY has just walked in*
26   *from work. He wears the sweater over his shoulders, "yuppie"*
27   *style. He is carrying his briefcase. KIERA pulls the ponytail out of*
28   *her hair. She looks bedraggled and worn out. She has a baby*
29   *blanket slung over her shoulder.)*
30   **RANDY: Hey, dear, how ya doing?**
31   **KIERA: Shhh. The baby's finally asleep.**
32   **RANDY:** *(Suggestively)* **Good. Then that means it's just the two of**
33   **us.**
34   **KIERA:** *(In her own world, ignoring his advances)* **Why doesn't she**
35   **sleep through the night? You remember Jenny from our**

1   Lamaze class?

2   RANDY: *(Playing with her hair)* **Huh? Was she the one who kept**

3   **hyperventilating during those breathing exercises and passing**

4   **out on the refreshment table?**

5   KIERA: **No, that was Angie. Jenny's the one who gained fifty-two**

6   **pounds.**

7   RANDY: **Oh. Yeah, I do remember her. Potato Chip Woman. The**

8   **one who could single-handedly clear off the refreshment table.**

9   KIERA: **Well, I saw her today at Wal-Mart, and she said her baby**

10   **has been sleeping through the night for the last six weeks!**

11   RANDY: **Huh** ... *(Leaning over to kiss her, trying to get romantic)*

12   KIERA: **Mary hasn't slept through the night yet!** *(Off-stage sound*

13   *of a baby starting to cry. The crying builds until the end of the*

14   *scene, when the wind blows again.)* **And neither have I.**

15   RANDY: **Kiera, you're ignoring me.**

16   KIERA: **Huh?**

17   RANDY: **Ignoring me. You're ignoring me.**

18   KIERA: **I'm just tired.** *(Starting to get up)* **I gotta get the baby.**

19   RANDY: *(Sighing, realizing he's not going to get what he wanted)* **I'll**

20   **get her this time. You stay here.**

21   KIERA: *(Calling to him as he leaves)* **Once she's out of diapers,**

22   **Randy** ... **I'll have more energy then. Then things will be**

23   **easier. Then we can spend more time together again, just you**

24   **and me** ... *(They freeze. Transition sound of wind blowing.*

25   *They're at the kitchen table again. RANDY has taken the sweater*

26   *off again. KIERA is balancing the checkbook and RANDY is*

27   *reading a magazine.)*

28   KIERA: **Randy! What's this check for seventy-eight dollars and**

29   **sixty-nine cents for?**

30   RANDY: **How should I know?**

31   KIERA: **Well, it's in your handwriting.**

32   RANDY: **How can you tell?**

33   KIERA: **Because I can't read it!** *(RANDY ignores her.)* **Randy!**

34   RANDY: **I don't know what it's for! OK?!**

35   KIERA: **The car needs new tires.**

1   RANDY: I know.

2   KIERA: And the rent was due on Tuesday.

3   RANDY: I know!

4   KIERA: And the lady from Mary's daycare called and said if we
5   don't start paying on time, she's not gonna be able to watch
6   her anymore. *(No response from RANDY.)* I thought with your
7   master's degree you were supposed to have all this job
8   security.

9   RANDY: Well, I guess not! Look, I'll find another position.

10 KIERA: But we moved away from our friends and our families. We
11   were supposed to start over here. A new life, remember? But
12   it's been tougher than ever.

13 RANDY: It's just a trend in the way the market is reacting to all the
14   new Internet stocks. I'll find a new job.

15 KIERA: *(After a pause)* We're not as close as we used to be, are we?

16 RANDY: I know. I'm not trying to be insensitive, but it's a lot of
17   work getting a career off the ground. Look, once I land a new
18   job, we can move out of this apartment, get a nice little house
19   in the suburbs ... Maybe I can look for a job near your
20   parents, OK?

21 KIERA: Really?

22 RANDY: Sure. Mary would love having Grandma and Grandpa
23   around ... Yeah. Then we'll be happy. We're just going
24   through a little slump ...

25 KIERA: You think so?

26 RANDY: Of course. *(They freeze. Transition sound of wind blowing.*
27   *Turn chairs slightly away from each other so their eyes don't meet.*
28   *Both are seated, pretending to drive in separate cars. They're*
29   *talking on cell phones, briefcase and purse by their sides.)*

30 KIERA: Randy?

31 RANDY: Hey, Kiera! Guess what? Yeah! I got some good news! You
32   know the Richardson proposal? Well, it went through! Yeah!
33   They loved us. And get this — Smithhouser said I shouldn't
34   get my hopes up necessarily — but when they were talking
35   new vice presidents, guess whose name came up?!

1 KIERA: Oh, that's great! What time are you gonna be home?
2 RANDY: I'm coming home early tonight so we can celebrate! No
3   more late nights at the office. I promise.
4 KIERA: OK, well, I'm picking Mary up from soccer practice, and
5   I was just gonna stop and get something to eat on the way.
6   And then I'm dropping her off at Lydia's while I go to the
7   PTA meeting.
8 RANDY: OK. Um, I'll see you later on, then!
9 KIERA: Congratulations.
10 RANDY: Thanks! ... Um, Kiera?
11 KIERA: Yeah?
12 RANDY: I really think there's some stuff we should talk about.
13 KIERA: I know, I know. I've been spread a little thin the last
14   couple months, but I'm gonna tell them at the PTA that I can't
15   serve as an officer again next year.
16 RANDY: And I've been working a lot —
17 KIERA: Don't worry, I think things will get easier soon.
18 RANDY: Maybe I could take a few days off next month. We could
19   go to the beach or something.
20 KIERA: I don't know, Randy. Who would watch Mary?
21 RANDY: I don't know —
22 KIERA: We'll see.
23 RANDY: Hey! Happy anniversary. Bet you thought I forgot, didn't
24   you?
25 KIERA: Happy anniversary. *(They freeze. Transition sound of wind*
26   *blowing. They're seated. He is eating cereal, she is drinking*
27   *coffee. They don't talk to each other. They each get up in turn, get*
28   *a cup of coffee and a piece of toast. Then they pass each other*
29   *without speaking. They have started to live their own separate*
30   *lives. They never make eye contact. Freeze. Transition sound of*
31   *wind blowing plays. Both are standing over the table where a pile*
32   *of papers rests.)*
33 RANDY: So it's all settled, huh?
34 KIERA: Yeah, all you need to do is sign.
35 RANDY: I get to see Mary every other weekend?

1   **KIERA:** Yeah, and for four weeks of the summer.

2   **RANDY:** Some way to celebrate our anniversary, huh?

3   **KIERA:** Yeah.

4   **RANDY:** *(Looking at the papers)* **What happened to us? We used to**

5   **be so close ... I really thought we were gonna make it.**

6   **KIERA:** **Yeah, so did I.** *(She picks up the piece of driftwood on the*

7   *table and looks at it.)* **So did I ...** *(As he reaches to sign, they*

8   *freeze; transition sound of wind blowing. Fadeout.)*

9

10

11

12

13

14

15

16

17

18

19

20

21

22

23

24

25

26

27

28

29

30

31

32

33

34

35

Homecoming

Summary: Chase lost money gambling. Again. When he returns home to try and work off his debts, his brother isn't too excited to see him.

Purpose: To show how easy it is to respond judgmentally rather than with grace.

Time: 4-6 minutes

Tone: Serious

Cast: Chase — A twentysomething guy addicted to gambling (male); Pete — His older, judgmental brother (male)

Props/Set: Grill and accessories, half-grilled steaks

Themes: Addictions, assumptions, compassion, family life, forgiveness, gambling, grace, grudges, home, judging, regrets, repentance, resentment, second chances

Text: "'My son,' the father said, 'you are always with me, and everything I have is yours. But we had to celebrate and be glad, because this brother of yours was dead and is alive again: he was lost and is found'" (Luke 15:32).

Notes: This modern-day version of Jesus' story of the Prodigal Son might not be immediately identifiable to your audience. It would work well to have someone read or recite Jesus' parable immediately after the sketch.

1   ***SETTING:*** The back yard at the homestead. As the scene opens, Pete
2   is grilling some steaks. Chase approaches.
3
4   **PETE:** Chase?
5   **CHASE:** Hey, Petey. How you doing?
6   **PETE:** Who let you in?
7   **CHASE:** The front door was locked and I smelled someone grilling
8   out. I came around the side of the house. Man, those steaks
9   look good.
10 **PETE:** I'm grilling them up for me and Mom. What are you doing
11   here? *(Sarcastically)* What — did you run out of money again?
12   Come back home to refuel for the next couple months?
13   *(CHASE is silent.)* Hmmm. By the looks of your clothes, I'd
14   guess you haven't won the lottery, yet. And oh, look at that ...
15   no watch. Where's the one Mom gave you when you started
16   college? Oh, I see. You probably needed to pay someone off,
17   huh? What was it this time? Off-track betting? Casinos?
18 **CHASE:** It's good to see you, too.
19 **PETE:** *(Sarcastically)* My little brother, the gambling man, stopping
20   by on his way to fame.
21 **CHASE:** I came home to stay.
22 **PETE:** *(Flipping a steak on the grill)* Yeah, whatever.
23 **CHASE:** Really.
24 **PETE:** Gimme a break. You came back for more money. It's not
25   like this is the first time.
26 **CHASE:** It's not like that this time.
27 **PETE:** Yeah, right.
28 **CHASE:** Um ... I'd really like to talk to Mom. Is she around?
29 **PETE:** She doesn't want to see you.
30 **CHASE:** What do you mean?
31 **PETE:** What do you think I mean? You lost all her savings! I can't
32   believe she keeps handing you more and more money to throw
33   away!
34 **CHASE:** Did she really say she didn't want to see me?
35 **PETE:** Look, she's not home, all right? *(Pausing to flip the meat)*

1   What did you want to tell her, anyway?

2   CHASE: Well, I'd rather tell her myself, in person.

3   PETE: I already told you — she doesn't want to see you ... So tell
4   me, and I'll pass the word along to her.

5   CHASE: Well —

6   PETE: Go on.

7   CHASE: I was going to say that I'm, uh ... sorry, and I want to
8   come back. Maybe work for her at the bookstore for a while.
9   Work off some of my debts —

10   PETE: *(Laughing)* After the way you talked to her?! You gotta be
11   kidding me! You told her you wished she were dead so you
12   could have your inheritance!

13   CHASE: *(Ashamed)* I know.

14   PETE: Do you really think she'd hire you to work in the store?

15   CHASE: I'm not sure, I —

16   PETE: Well, I wouldn't, that's for sure. I wouldn't give you
17   another penny.

18   CHASE: I know.

19   PETE: What's that supposed to mean?

20   CHASE: Just that you always give people what they deserve.
21   Nothing more, nothing less.

22   PETE: That's right — I do. Let 'em earn their keep. Give them
23   what they deserve. And you don't deserve anything ...
24   Flunking out of college after one semester, betting on
25   everything that moves —

26   CHASE: *(Motioning to PETE)* Keep going. I deserve it.

27   PETE: Hang on ... wait a minute. Listen, I might be able to
28   arrange something ... maybe talk to Mom for you, soften
29   things up a little. You know, put the good word in ... Maybe I
30   could even find a position for you ... for a price. How much of
31   that money from last time do you still have left?

32   CHASE: None of it. It's gone. It's all gone. *(Hanging his head in*
33   *shame)*

34   PETE: What? All of it? I can't believe it! You wasted it all! And
35   then you come waltzing back in here, expecting us to welcome

1   you home with open arms? Fat chance. Trust is something you
2   gotta earn, little brother. Trust is something you gotta earn!
3 CHASE: I knew you'd say that. That's why I was looking for Mom.
4   *(Freeze. Fadeout.)*
5
6
7
8
9
10
11
12
13
14
15
16
17
18
19
20
21
22
23
24
25
26
27
28
29
30
31
32
33
34
35

Moving In

Summary: When Brenda finds out about Cici's drug problem, she offers to help. But will Cici just continue making excuses and hiding?

Purpose: To reveal that God accepts us "as is" and will work to remodel our lives.

Time: 6-8 minutes

Tone: Serious

Cast: Cici — An unbelieving nurse with something to hide (female); Brenda — Her Christian friend (female)

Props/Set: Packing tape, large cardboard boxes, three sweaters, photographs of a house, a syringe, papers, goofy-looking lamp, coffee table

Themes: Addictions, appearances, authenticity, conversion, excuses, forgiveness, grace, hiding, Jesus, misconceptions about Christianity, new life, relationships, repentance, second chances, secrets, witnessing

Text: "Being confident of this, that he who began a good work in you will carry it on to completion until the day of Christ Jesus" (Philippians 1:6).

Notes: This is one of the most evangelistic sketches in the book. It ends with Cici acknowledging her sin and her need for Christ. Be sensitive to focusing the emotions of the actors into the action so the scene doesn't come across as preachy.

1	***SETTING:*** *Cici's living room. There are piles of boxes all around. It's*
2	*obvious she is packing to move.*
3	
4	**BRENDA: Hey, Cici? You in there?**
5	**CICI: Yeah! I'm over here! Behind all these boxes!**
6	**BRENDA:** *(Crossing Stage Right toward her)* **Oh, there you are!**
7	*(They hug.)* **Look at all this stuff!**
8	**CICI: Yeah, and this is only part of it. Andy already took two loads**
9	**over. You never realize how much junk you have until you try**
10	**to move it all.**
11	**BRENDA: I can't believe you guys are really moving.**
12	**CICI:** *(Overwhelmed and slightly sad)* **Me neither.**
13	**BRENDA: I'm excited for you, though. Well ... what can I help you**
14	**with?**
15	**CICI: I guess you can help me tape these boxes of dishes shut. Andy**
16	**took the moving van, and I've got all this fragile stuff left I**
17	**need to take over in the Suburban ...**
18	**BRENDA:** *(Noticing some photos lying on the table)* **Hey, are those**
19	**pictures of your new house?**
20	**CICI: Yeah!** *(Hands them to BRENDA.)*
21	**BRENDA: Wow! The place looks great!**
22	**CICI: It looks good now, but you should have seen it before we**
23	**fixed it up.**
24	**BRENDA: Pretty bad, huh?**
25	**CICI: Are you kidding? It was falling apart. Doors hanging off the**
26	**hinges and broken windows. It needed to be painted and**
27	**rewired. The people who lived there before had all these cats,**
28	**and the smell was terrible! Andy's been spending every**
29	**weekend over there for the last two months.**
30	**BRENDA: Wow.**
31	**CICI:** *(Motioning to the pictures)* **Go on, you can keep 'em. I've got**
32	**doubles. They can remind you of me after I'm gone ... Oh! I**
33	**almost forgot! I'll get those sweaters you lent me.**
34	**BRENDA: Oh, don't even worry about them.**
35	**CICI: No, c'mon. I wanna return them.** *(As they move across the*

1   *stage)* **I'm really gonna miss you, Brenda.**

2   **BRENDA: I'm gonna miss you, too, Cici.**

3   **CICI: You've really been there for me this last year. It hasn't been**

4   **easy, you know ...**

5   **BRENDA: I know.** *(Awkward silence)* **Um ... Were you able to find**

6   **a new job in _____?** *(Insert the name of a nearby state.)*

7   **CICI: No — which is no surprise. Andy got a pretty good job,**

8   **though. I guess I won't be going back to work for a while. I'm**

9   **supposed to start going to these** *(Sarcastically)* **support group**

10   **meetings ...** *(Searching for the sweaters)* **Now where's the box**

11   **with those sweaters?**

12   **BRENDA: Oh, Cici! There's that lamp you bought last fall when**

13   **we went to the flea market down on Highway 81** *(Or the name*

14   *of a familiar street).* **Remember the look on Andy's face when**

15   **you brought it home?**

16   **CICI:** *(Still rummaging)* **Yeah. How could I forget?**

17   **BRENDA:** *(Distracted, still remembering)* **And then that night, we**

18   **all went back to the hospital together for the Halloween**

19   **party ... Remember? For all the nursing staff? Dr. Jacobs was**

20   **pretending to be a river dancer ...**

21   **CICI:** *(Pulling out a sweater)* **Here you go, Brenda ... At least now**

22   **no one can say I stole anything from you.**

23   **BRENDA: What?**

24   **CICI: Stole, you know, took what wasn't mine.**

25   **BRENDA: Oh, Cici. Listen ... I'm sorry. I forgot —** *(CICI is silent.)*

26   **Listen, I know it's been tough ever since —**

27   **CICI: Ever since what? I got fired. Just say it: Cici Williams got**

28   **fired from the hospital for taking syringes out of the supply**

29   **cabinet. Well, I didn't do it, OK?**

30   **BRENDA: OK.**

31   **CICI: It was an inventory mistake.**

32   **BRENDA: All right.**

33   **CICI: I mean, one false accusation, and they can ruin your whole**

34   **life!** *(Handing her the sweater)*

35   **BRENDA: Yeah ...** *(Changing the subject)* **Oh! I forgot all about**

1 **this one!** *(She takes a sweater and unfolds it to look at it, and a*
2 *syringe falls out.)* **Oh, what's that?**
3 **CICI: Nothing. It's, um —**
4 **BRENDA:** *(Picking it up)* **It's a syringe ...**
5 **CICI: Somebody must have put that in my drawer.**
6 **BRENDA: It** *was* **you.**
7 **CICI: No!**
8 **BRENDA: You did do it. And all this time you've been telling me**
9 **you didn't!**
10 **CICI:** *(Finally giving in)* **OK, look, it happened once. But I don't**
11 **have a problem or anything.**
12 **BRENDA: Cici, don't lie to me. We've been friends for a long time —**
13 **CICI: Really! I was just depressed after our miscarriage, and I just**
14 **needed something to help kill the pain —**
15 **BRENDA: How long?**
16 **CICI: A couple months. Maybe six.**
17 **BRENDA: That's why you always wear long sleeves.** *(Silence from*
18 *CICI.)* **And why you've been so moody and irritable.**
19 **CICI: You can't tell anyone!**
20 **BRENDA: And now you're moving ...**
21 **CICI: Yeah. How did Andy put it? "We can start over. Make a clean**
22 **break. A fresh start."**
23 **BRENDA: But you're not gonna stop, are you?** *(More silence from*
24 *CICI)* **You're not.**
25 **CICI:** *(Without looking her in the face)* **Maybe you should go now.**
26 **I've got a lot of packing to do.**
27 **BRENDA: Cici, let me help you.**
28 **CICI: Please leave. You'd never understand what it's like!**
29 **BRENDA: What do you mean?**
30 **CICI: Your life! It's ... so perfect. You've got a husband who**
31 **doesn't cheat on you, great kids, a nice little house. We'd been**
32 **trying to have kids for three years! And then when I**
33 **miscarried, Andy became really distant ... and then with**
34 **everything at work ...**
35 **BRENDA: My life's not as perfect as it seems. Remember I told you**

1   I became a Christian a few years ago?

2   CICI: Yeah. So?

3   BRENDA: OK, well, that's when the remodeling began.

4   CICI: What do you mean?

5   BRENDA: My first marriage was a disaster. I started drinking.

6   CICI: I didn't know that.

7   BRENDA: Yeah. I saw a counselor for three years afterward. I still

8   haven't totally recovered from everything. I probably never

9   will. But God's been remodeling my life ever since.

10   CICI: But Brenda, don't you understand? That wasn't the first

11   time. It was just the first time I got caught! Why would God

12   be interested in me?

13 BRENDA: *(Reaching out to take her arm)* Cici, God forgives you

14   for that.

15 CICI: *(Defeated)* You must not know me as well as you think you

16   do. I'm just not good enough ...

17 BRENDA: *(Sticking her hand in her purse for a tissue, she grabs the*

18   *picture as well. Suddenly she has an idea.)* Why did you and

19   Andy decide to fix up the house before moving in?

20 CICI: *(Taking the tissue)* What do you mean? Who would want to

21   live in a run-down place like that?

22 BRENDA: I can only think of one person.

23 CICI: Who?

24 BRENDA: A carpenter. One who loves moving into rundown

25   places and fixing them up.

26 CICI: *(After a moment, beginning to understand)* You mean Jesus?

27   Trusting in him? Is that who you're talking about?

28 BRENDA: Yeah. Remodeling from the inside out. You don't have

29   to change first, Cici. He'll worry about that. All you have to

30   do is invite him in to stay.

31 CICI: I'm just not good enough.

32 BRENDA: None of us are. That's the whole point. You just need to

33   be willing to change.

34 CICI: *(Genuinely)* Willing to change, huh? Brenda, I'd like to let

35   him in ... that is, if he's willing to have me. But how? How do

1   **I open the door?**
2 **BRENDA:** *(Placing her hand on CICI's shoulder)* **I think you just**
3   **did.** *(Freeze. Fadeout.)*
4
5
6
7
8
9
10
11
12
13
14
15
16
17
18
19
20
21
22
23
24
25
26
27
28
29
30
31
32
33
34
35

Remembering Emily

Summary: Layla is looking for an old high school classmate that no one seems to remember. Finally Whitney remembers her, but she doesn't share the news Layla was hoping to hear.

Purpose: To explore how choices have lasting consequences.

Time: 6-8 minutes

Tone: Serious with lighthearted moments

Cast: Layla — A woman with some regrets (female); Whitney — Her ex-cheerleader friend (female)

Props/Set: High school yearbook, a refreshment table with crackers and chips and soda

Themes: Abuse, consequences, gossip, guilt, regrets, relationships, second chances, stereotypes, suicide

Text: "He will reply, 'I tell you the truth, whatever you did not do for one of the least of these, you did not do for me'" (Matthew 25:45).

Notes: Layla is thoughtful and a little shy. Whitney is bubbly and outgoing. Let the actors eat and drink from the refreshment table behind them.

1 ***SETTING:*** A gymnasium at Westside High, Layla's and Whitney's old
2 high school. They've come back for their ten-year class reunion.
3
4 **LAYLA:** *(Carrying the yearbook, talking to an imaginary person)* **Hey,**
5 **Charles! Good to see you, too! Yeah, go Westside High!**
6 *(Turning to the refreshment table, sighing, talking to herself)*
7 **Where is she? I wonder if she even showed up.** *(Gets a small*
8 *snack plate as WHITNEY enters.)*
9 **WHITNEY:** *(Entering)* **Layla? Layla Schneider?**
10 **LAYLA:** *(Turning to see her)* **Whitney? Is that you?** *(They hug, and*
11 *WHITNEY is overly bubbly.)*
12 **WHITNEY: It's so great to see you!**
13 **LAYLA: You, too!**
14 **WHITNEY: Can you believe it? Ten years! It's gone by so fast!**
15 **LAYLA: No kidding.**
16 **WHITNEY: You look good! Have you been working out?**
17 **LAYLA: I still run a couple times a week. But look at you, you look**
18 **great!**
19 **WHITNEY: Well, you know what they say — old cheerleaders**
20 **never die, they just become aerobics instructors.** *(Doing a*
21 *cheer)* **Who's the team with the gold and green? Westside**
22 **High, Westside High! Who's the team with the scorin'**
23 **machine? Westside High, Westside High! Yeah!**
24 **LAYLA:** *(Warmly)* **They don't do cheers like that anymore; it's all**
25 **this robotic-looking stuff.**
26 **WHITNEY: I know, like ...** *(Miming modern cheerleading)*
27 **LAYLA: That's pretty good. So how are you?**
28 **WHITNEY: I'm great! I wasn't kidding before. I do teach aerobics**
29 **at the Bulk-n-Tone Gym down on Fort Henry Drive** *(Or a local*
30 *gym)*. **How about you?**
31 **LAYLA: I went on to college. Studied communication. I work**
32 **twenty hours a week doing marketing for a long distance**
33 **company** *(Or a local newspaper or media company)*. **That, and**
34 **I'm a mom.**
35 **WHITNEY: Oh, so you have kids?**

1   LAYLA: Yeah, two boys.

2   WHITNEY: Wow! I bet they're a handful.

3   LAYLA: Sometimes. What about you? Any kids?

4   WHITNEY: No. I was married for a couple years, but you know,

5   he was a jerk ... what can I say? No kids. Now I'm back to

6   playing the field ... Did you see Chuck Warren? He's put on

7   like two hundred and fifty pounds!

8   LAYLA: Little Chucky ... I know, I didn't even recognize him.

9   WHITNEY: And Gary Wilkerson is still gorgeous. I talked to him.

10 LAYLA: What's he doing these days?

11 WHITNEY: Well, let's see. He just got divorced from wife number

12   three, teaches tennis lessons at "the club" and vacations in

13   Bermuda.

14 LAYLA: Wow.

15 WHITNEY: Doesn't sound too bad, huh?

16 LAYLA: I'm pretty much set as far as husbands go. *(Eating her*

17   *snacks, unsure of what else to say)* These are good chips.

18 WHITNEY: Remember how you used to come over to my house in

19   high school, and we'd stay up all night eating Cheetos and

20   pizza and talking about —

21 LAYLA: Phil Parker! Ew. I can't believe we were interested in

22   him!

23 WHITNEY: We? The way I remember it, girl, it was you. And you

24   would have done anything to go out with him!

25 LAYLA: Oh yeah? Well, remember that pink dress you bought to

26   try and get his attention?

27 WHITNEY: Yeah. My dad wouldn't let me out of the house in it!

28   He said it was so short, it left nothing to the imagination ...

29 LAYLA: Phil would have liked it —

30 WHITNEY: He would have liked it too much ...

31 LAYLA: Did you see him here?

32 WHITNEY: Yeah, he's here with his cute little wife. Oh well ...

33 LAYLA: Hey, remember that time a bunch of us from my church

34   came over to your house to swim, and that little green snake

35   got into the pool?

1   WHITNEY: Little! That thing was at least seven inches long! I
2   thought that one girl was gonna scream forever!
3   LAYLA: Yeah, Emily —
4   WHITNEY: Was that her name? Emily? Anyway, she must have
5   really hated snakes … *(Gesturing)* Hey, is that what I think it is?
6   LAYLA: My yearbook? Yeah. I brought it along.
7   WHITNEY: Wow! What a great idea!
8   LAYLA: Yeah, there was someone I was hoping could sign it.
9   WHITNEY: Who?
10   LAYLA: That girl — Emily.
11   WHITNEY: Emily? From the pool?
12   LAYLA: Yeah.
13   WHITNEY: What's her last name?
14   LAYLA: Chambers … Do you remember her?
15   WHITNEY: Oh … Hmmm … Not really.
16   LAYLA: Nobody does! I've asked half the people here if they've
17   seen her, and it's like she didn't even exist.
18   WHITNEY: What did she do?
19   LAYLA: You mean like cheerleading and stuff?
20   WHITNEY: Yeah.
21   LAYLA: I don't know. I don't think she did anything.
22   WHITNEY: Was she your friend?
23   LAYLA: Not really.
24   WHITNEY: Then why are you looking for her?
25   LAYLA: I went to school with her for four years. She went to my
26   church. And all I really remember was seeing her screaming
27   by the pool that day, and everyone sitting around laughing.
28   It's like she was invisible, and that day, the only day I really
29   remember, she was terrified, and we laughed at her.
30   WHITNEY: I never thought of that before.
31   LAYLA: Yeah. It wasn't that we made fun of her, it's that we didn't
32   notice her … Last month one of my boys went to camp for the
33   first time, and he had a terrible week.
34   WHITNEY: Oh, no! What happened?
35   LAYLA: Well, most of the kids in his cabin all knew each other, and

1   he felt left out. He told me when we were driving home, "I

2   wouldn't have cared if they made fun of me. But they just

3   ignored me, Mom. I'd rather be picked on than ignored."

4   WHITNEY: Wow.

5   LAYLA: I know. But that was only one week. Think of what it must

6   have been like for Emily, year after year.

7   WHITNEY: *(Deep sigh)* Well …

8   LAYLA: We ignored her, Whitney. Until she screamed — and then

9   we laughed. Anyway, when I found my yearbook I thought of

10   her, because the last time I saw her was when everyone was

11   signing yearbooks. She came running over to have me sign her

12   book … but the thing was … it was empty.

13   WHITNEY: What do you mean it was empty?

14   LAYLA: No one else had signed it.

15   WHITNEY: No one?

16   LAYLA: Nope. So I signed it and put something like, "To a good

17   friend from church, Love always, Layla." And then she smiled

18   really big and said, "Thanks, Layla! You've been a great

19   friend, can I sign your book, too?" But my book was being

20   passed around, you know. So I told her she could sign it, but

21   then her mom drove up and she had to leave. She turned to

22   me and said, "Maybe next time I see you I can sign it! I won't

23   forget you. Good-bye, Layla!" I figured there'd be another

24   chance. But I never saw her again … She told me I'd been a

25   great friend.

26   WHITNEY: What did you say her last name was?

27   LAYLA: Chambers.

28   WHITNEY: *(Thinking)* Chambers … Chambers …

29   LAYLA: *(Opening her yearbook)* Yeah. See? Here's her picture.

30   WHITNEY: Wait a minute … *(Seriously)* Oh, no.

31   LAYLA: What?

32   WHITNEY: You aren't gonna believe this. I do remember her.

33   LAYLA: *(Looking around)* Have you seen her? Is she here?

34   WHITNEY: No.

35   LAYLA: What do you remember?

1   **WHITNEY: That picture. That's the one they used in the paper.**

2   **LAYLA: What do you mean?**

3   **WHITNEY: It never occurred to me —**

4   **LAYLA: What are you talking about?**

5   **WHITNEY: She stayed here in town. They found her in her**

6   **apartment a couple years after high school. She'd, you know —**

7   **LAYLA: What?**

8   **WHITNEY: You know ... taken a whole bottle of pills.**

9   **LAYLA:** *(Shocked and in despair)* **No ... Are you sure it was her?**

10   **WHITNEY: Yeah. I remember it because it said Westside High in**

11   **the headlines, and that's what caught my attention,** *(Pointing)*

12   **and that's the picture. It was her.**

13   **LAYLA: She killed herself?**

14   **WHITNEY: I guess so. I'm really sorry ...**

15   **LAYLA:** *(Staring at the book)* **Yeah, me too ... You don't remember**

16   **ever having her in class or anything?**

17   **WHITNEY: All I really remember is that day by the pool when she**

18   **screamed —**

19   **LAYLA: — And we laughed.**

20   **WHITNEY: Yeah, we laughed ...** *(After an awkward pause)* **Um ...**

21   **listen, I was hoping to meet up with Gary one more time**

22   **before he takes off ... You don't mind if I slip out ...**

23   **LAYLA: No ...**

24   **WHITNEY: I don't mean to be insensitive or anything.**

25   **LAYLA: It's OK.**

26   **WHITNEY: I'll see you a little later, OK?**

27   **LAYLA:** *(Still staring at the book)* **OK.**

28   **WHITNEY: Hey, sorry you didn't find her ...** *(Turns to exit.)*

29   **LAYLA:** *(Touching her face in the yearbook)* **I'm sorry I waited so**

30   **long to look ... Good-bye, Emily. Good-bye ...** *(Closes*

31   *yearbook and freezes. Fadeout.)*

32

33

34

35

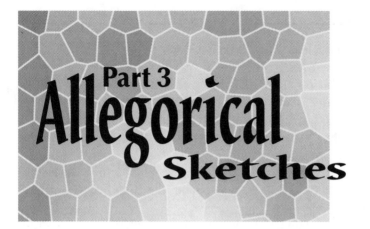

Part 3
Allegorical
Sketches

"Wait a minute ... Did you get that?"

"No, did you?"

*"No, but I don't think it was just a story about a farmer ...
Let's ask Jesus what it means."*

When Jesus finished his story of the four different types of
soil (Matthew 13:1-9), his followers knew that below the surface
there was something else going on.

So they asked him to explain the parable to them, and only
then did they begin to understand the significance of the
symbolism in his teaching.

While contemporary sketches work well to expose issues,
allegorical sketches serve best to explore connections. Jesus
explained that his parables were for his followers — that not
everyone would understand them. By the same token, the sketches
in this section may be more understandable and identifiable to
believers than seekers.

Even though many of these present contemporary situations,
two stories are going on at once. In the previous section, things
were pretty much what they appeared to be. Now we enter the
world where things are a bit more symbolic.

As each sketch unfolds, the audience will begin to see that the
story they're watching is not really what it appears to be. The
impact comes from the parallel between two apparently unrelated
ideas.

The Hippo Critics

Summary: When Fred doesn't respond to God's invitation to get on the ark, he and his wife Marge are left behind.

Purpose: To reveal how some people are left out of God's blessings because of unbelief and hypocrisy.

Time: 5-7 minutes

Tone: Lighthearted until the end

Cast: Marge — A gossiping hippopotamus (female); Fred — Her judgmental husband (male); Voiceover — Reader of the opening narration (could be Fred)

Props/Set: A curtained-off area of the stage, long blades of grass for the hippos to chew (made of paper)

Themes: Consequences, faith, gossip, grace, judging, stereotypes, trust

Text: "Jesus replied: 'A certain man was preparing a great banquet and invited many guests. At the time of the banquet he sent his servant to tell those who had been invited, "Come, for everything is now ready." But they all alike began to make excuses'" (Luke 14:16-18a).

Notes: This sketch is a little absurd because Fred and Marge are hippos. However, the hippos' response to God's invitation echoes the response of many people today. As Fred says, "Nothing's for free, Marge. Nothing." You can either have one of the actors do the opening voiceover or have another person read it from Off-stage. During the sketch, the audience should only see two heads On-stage. The rest of Fred and Marge's bodies are hidden behind a curtain.

1   **SETTING**: A marsh prior to The Flood. After the voiceover intro, all
2   the audience sees are the two heads of Marge and Fred On-stage.
3
4   **VOICEOVER: Marge and Fred Hippopotamus stood staring at the**
5   **long line of animals in front of them. Two of every kind of**
6   **creature in the jungle were walking, hopping, crawling,**
7   **slithering, galloping, or fluttering past their swimming hole.**
8   *(MARGE and FRED's heads appear.)*
9   **MARGE:** *(Chewing a blade of grass)* **They've all gone wacko, Fred.**
10   **Completely wacko!**
11   **FRED: I'll say they have, Marge. You might have expected as much**
12   **from the weasels,** *(Nodding to the side)* **but not the rabbits!**
13   **They were always such a nice couple. A little too amorous, but**
14   **nice.**
15   **MARGE:** *(Nodding in agreement, chewing a mouthful of grass)* **Not**
16   **just the rabbits, Fred! Look!**
17   **FRED: Well, I'll be … If it isn't two snakes in the grass. I would**
18   **never have thought it — and the zebras, too! Look at that!**
19   **Always following the crowd, they are. Always trying to blend**
20   **in with the herd. Everything's so black and white for them …**
21   **and in such a hurry! Did you hear where they're all going?**
22   **MARGE: That's the weirdest thing of all. They're heading toward**
23   **a building in the middle of the desert. I heard one of the**
24   **panthers call it an "ark."**
25   **FRED: A "nark"? What's a nark? Like a lark? Or an aardvark or**
26   **something?**
27   **MARGE: No, not a nark, Fred. An ark. And it's not a bird or an**
28   **aardvark, it's something that's supposed to float … like this.**
29   *(Pretends to float by moving head back and forth.)*
30   **FRED:** *(Watching her)* **Very nice. But why are they all heading to the**
31   **nark?**
32   **MARGE: Ark. And I'm not sure. Something having to do with a big**
33   **flood.**
34   **FRED: Hey! Look! There go the 'gators. Just married last week,**
35   **and already off to honeymoon on a nark. Too bad they don't**

1 have brains as large as they do mouths.

2 MARGE: It's too bad so many of our friends are so gullible.

3 FRED: You could say that again, Marge. Gullible and stupid. Look,
4 there go the lions! I can't believe it. I always thought they had
5 more sense than to go chasing after a floating aardvark!

6 MARGE: Ark, Fred. Ark.

7 FRED: Oh, yeah — well, whatever. Sir Lion, for all his roar,
8 certainly has a rather small amount of willpower. He should
9 stand on his own and do his own thing rather than just going
10 along with the rest of the animals. You'd think this was a
11 stampede or something! Maybe he is the coward the hyenas
12 are always saying he is. You know what I heard? I heard he —

13 MARGE: *(Interrupting him)* Fred, do you think there is anything to
14 this flood business?

15 FRED: *(Shocked)* Are you kidding me? Does it look like it's gonna
16 rain? And why head to the middle of the desert and not high
17 ground? And who ever heard of an alligator being afraid of a
18 little rain? It's not logical, Marge! I'm glad that at least I have
19 more sense than my dim-witted neighbors. For example, I got
20 an invitation a few weeks ago to take you on a free trip.

21 MARGE: You did?!

22 FRED: Sure. "Exotic Newlywed Cruise," it said. "Take your wife
23 on a cruise around the world. Free! No strings attached!"
24 Must have been this nark thing. I just threw it away.
25 Nothing's for free, Marge. Nothing.

26 MARGE: *(Letting all that soak in)* So they must have gotten the
27 invitation too.

28 FRED: Yeah, and look at them! Scurrying around as if it were the
29 end of the world!

30 MARGE: I wonder who sent out those invitations.

31 FRED: Who knows? *(Hands himself a blade of grass from behind the
32 curtain and begins to chew it.)*

33 MARGE: *(After a pause)* Fred! You're not going to believe this. I
34 just saw Hilda and Henry walking toward the ark!

35 FRED: *(Looking up)* Hilda and Henry Hippopotamus?

1   **MARGE: Yes! Look!** *(Nodding to the side)*
2   **FRED: Sure enough, Marge, you're right. I never thought it would**
3   **come to this. Wait 'til I tell the guys at the watering hole.**
4   *(Peering to the side)* **Well, it looks like that's the last of them.**
5   **Poor creatures. Listen, I'm gonna go wallow for a while. See**
6   **you back at home.**
7   **MARGE: OK, Fred. See you at home ... Um, Fred, do you see those**
8   **clouds?**
9   **FRED:** *(Peering at the sky)* **Well, how about that?! Looks like a little**
10   **storm is moving in. Ha, maybe this is the big flood!** *(Chuckling)*
11   **You know what, Marge? Someday our grandkids are gonna**
12   **look back at this and laugh at all those fools for running after**
13   **that nark.**
14   **MARGE: Yeah, I guess so. Listen, Fred, it's starting to rain. I'm**
15   **going under for a while.** *(She exits by ducking her head down.)*
16   **FRED:** *(Watching her go)* **OK, see you later, alligator — ha, ha —**
17   **just kidding, just kidding ...** *(He exits by ducking his head*
18   *down. Fadeout.)*
19
20
21
22
23
24
25
26
27
28
29
30
31
32
33
34
35

The Operation

Summary: Wally is about to discover that the cure for his chest pains is trusting his doctor's advice.

Purpose: To demonstrate that we are saved solely through faith and that God wants us to share that good news with others.

Time: 3-5 minutes

Tone: Lighthearted

Cast: Wally — A nervous and edgy patient hoping for good news (male); Dan — His caring and benevolent doctor (male)

Props/Set: Stethoscope, doctor's scrubs, exam table

Themes: Choices, conversion, faith, God's power, grace, new life, repentance, spiritual health, trust, witnessing

Text: "I will give you a new heart and put a new spirit in you; I will remove from you your heart of stone and give you a heart of flesh" (Ezekiel 36:26).

Notes: This script will go well with a message about evangelism, God's grace, or saving faith. You could change the names and make either or both characters female.

1   *SETTING:* A doctor's exam room where Dan has just finished
2   examining Wally. As Wally is buttoning up his shirt, Dan prepares
3   to tell him some important news.
4
5   **WALLY:** *(Nervously buttoning up his shirt)* **Well, what's the word,**
6   **Doc?**
7   **DAN:** *(Folding up stethoscope)* **Well, there's some good news and**
8   **some bad news.**
9   **WALLY: Well, give me the good news first!**
10   **DAN: The good news is I've seen this condition before — many**
11   **times before — and I've treated it successfully every time —**
12   **WALLY: Oh, that's a relief.**
13   **DAN: — The patient has gone into surgery.**
14   **WALLY: Surgery!**
15   **DAN: Yes, surgery.**
16   **WALLY:** *(Stammering)* **But Doc … what's the bad news?**
17   **DAN: The bad news is that you have a heart of stone.**
18   **WALLY: What? A heart of stone?**
19   **DAN: That's right — a boulder the size of your shoulder. A**
20   **genuine, one hundred percent fossilized heart of stone.**
21   **WALLY: But Doc, how can that be?**
22   **DAN: It's a natural condition. You were born that way.**
23   **WALLY:** *(Rubbing or clutching chest)* **That doesn't make any sense.**
24   **I've never heard of anyone having a heart of stone before …**
25   **DAN: That's why I'm the doctor and you're the patient.**
26   **WALLY: You're serious?**
27   **DAN: Serious. And that's why you've been having those terrible**
28   **chest pains.**
29   **WALLY: But what can be done about it? How do you treat it?**
30   **DAN: A complete heart transplant. Out with the old, in with the**
31   **new. It's the only way.**
32   **WALLY:** *(Gulping and nervous)* **How successful is the surgery? How**
33   **have the other people done after their transplants?**
34   **DAN: They've had good times and bad times, easy times and hard**
35   **times, but the transplant has always taken. Not one of them**

1 has ever died of heart disease.

2 WALLY: But a complete transplant ... that seems kind of drastic,
3   don't you think? I mean, I've had this heart ever since I was
4   born.

5 DAN: And you'll have it when you die unless you let me give you a
6   transplant.

7 WALLY: Couldn't you replace part of it and leave the rest?

8 DAN: Nope. I operate entirely on the "wholehearted" principle.

9 WALLY: Doc, maybe you made a mistake, I mean, maybe I should
10   get a second opinion.

11 DAN: Go right ahead, but before you do, I should warn you about
12   something.

13 WALLY: What's that?

14 DAN: There are a whole lot of doctors out there, but I'm the only
15   one who specializes in transplanting hearts of stone.

16 WALLY: The only one?

17 DAN: Yes.

18 WALLY: What do the other doctors do?

19 DAN: You name it, they do it. Plastic surgery, kidney stones, gall
20   bladders, some even specialize in replacing lost underarm
21   hair. Sure, some *claim* to be heart doctors, but in every case
22   their operations have ended in fatality.

23 WALLY: Fatality! You mean their patients died?

24 DAN: Yes. Death does tend to be fatal.

25 WALLY: Well, maybe it's not really a heart of stone. I mean ...
26   maybe you made a mistake.

27 DAN: It'd be my first one.

28 WALLY: Look, Doc. OK ... how much time do I have left?

29 DAN: I rarely make those kinds of predictions for people. But let
30   me put it this way: Without a new heart, you could be stone-
31   cold any day.

32 WALLY: Any day?

33 DAN: That's right.

34 WALLY: When do I need to decide whether or not to have the
35   operation?

1   DAN: Well, my friend, you have all the information you need. If
2   you decide you don't want to have the operation, it could
3   mean only one thing.
4   WALLY: What's that?
5   DAN: *(Pausing and staring straight at WALLY)* It could only mean
6   that you don't believe what I'm telling you. You don't trust
7   me. If you believed me, you would follow my advice. It would
8   be your unbelief alone that would cause your death. *(As their*
9   *eyes meet, there is a moment of intense silence.)*
10   WALLY: Doc, I do believe you can complete the operation
11   successfully. I'm just kind of scared. *(Swallowing hard)* Is there
12   any way you could help me trust you more? *(DAN begins to*
13   *smile.)* Hey — why are you smiling? What's so funny?
14   DAN: That wasn't so bad, now was it?
15   WALLY: What wasn't so bad?
16   DAN: The operation.
17   WALLY: Operation? What operation? *(WALLY looks down at his*
18   *chest and is amazed to see it rise and fall so smoothly. He takes a*
19   *few deep breaths and pats his chest a few times to make sure it's*
20   *for real. His chest pains are gone! A smile sweeps across his face.)*
21   WALLY: Doc, I don't know how you did it! I feel like a new person!
22   How can I ever thank you?
23   DAN: You're welcome. And as far as thanks, I just ask for one
24   thing.
25   WALLY: Anything, Doc, you name it!
26   DAN: Recommend me to your friends. *(They freeze. Blackout.)*
27
28
29
30
31
32
33
34
35

Information ... Please!

Summary: When Vivian enters the library, she is looking for someone to teach her how to read. Unfortunately for her, this library has no one to help her.

Purpose: To show the necessity for Christians to work together and minister in unity.

Time: 4-6 minutes

Tone: Lighthearted until the end

Cast: Vivian — A curious and confused lady looking for help (female); Darren — A "know-it-all" employee (male)

Props/Set: Books, papers, computer keyboard, countertop

Themes: Assumptions, church issues, divisiveness, missions, unity

Text: "I have given them the glory that you gave me, that they may be one as we are one: I in them and you in me. May they be brought to complete unity to let the world know that you sent me and have loved them even as you have loved me" (John 17:22-23).

Notes: As you rehearse this sketch, remember that the audience will slowly be catching on to the fact that it is a parable about how Christians have treated each other. If your church is full of people who have grown up going to church, this may be a sensitive area. If your congregation tends to include more seekers or visitors, they may find the sketch funnier as they realize you are addressing one of the things that kept them away from church for so long.

1   *SETTING:* An information desk at a library. As the scene opens,
2   Darren is behind the reference desk typing on a computer
3   keyboard or sorting some books. Vivian enters, looking a little
4   curious and confused.
5
6   VIVIAN: Excuse me, sir?
7   DARREN: *(Speaking in an "uppity" English accent)* **Yes ma'am, how**
8   **may I help you?**
9   VIVIAN: **Well, I'm new to the area, and I've been driving around,**
10   **and it seems to me there are a lot of libraries here in this town.**
11 DARREN: **Yes, fifty-two to be exact.**
12 VIVIAN: **Well, doesn't this town only have a thousand people?**
13 DARREN: **Yes, ma'am. Well, nine hundred twenty-eight to be**
14   **exact, according to the latest census.**
15 VIVIAN: **OK, but why are there so many libraries?**
16 DARREN: **Well, a long time ago, there was only one library in**
17   **town. But throughout the years, there have been quite a few**
18   **library splits.**
19 VIVIAN: **Library splits? What are those?**
20 DARREN: **A library split occurs whenever there's a difference of**
21   **opinion over what books to stock, what services to offer, how**
22   **much fines should be … You know, things like that.**
23 VIVIAN: **Hmmm.**
24 DARREN: **Some people say one thing, others another, and pretty**
25   **soon no one is happy. So some of the staff leave to start their**
26   **own library down the block. Sometimes when people don't**
27   **like the librarian at a certain facility, they leave and find a**
28   **librarian who runs the library more like they would run it if**
29   **they were in charge. Over the years different management**
30   **theories and approaches have been tried, resulting in more**
31   **and more library splits.**
32 VIVIAN: **What do you mean?**
33 DARREN: **Well, for example, some librarians believe you should**
34   **make the library as accessible as possible. We call them the**
35   **"library growth" crowd. They build big parking lots, have**

1   friendly greeters, reader-of-the-month clubs, and welcoming
2   committees. Other librarians belong to the "field-book of
3   dreams" crowd.
4   VIVIAN: The "field-book of dreams"?
5   DARREN: Yes: "If you build it, they will come." They believe if you
6   just build a library, then everyone who is interested in a book
7   will seek out your library, find the book, and check it out
8   without any help.
9   VIVIAN: Wait a minute. I don't mean to interrupt, but aren't all
10   the libraries working toward the same goal?
11   DARREN: Encouraging people to read? *(Hesitating slightly)* Well,
12   yes. But some librarians believe that should be done through
13   the Internet and multimedia, others through magazines and
14   journals, others through novels, newspapers, and trade books,
15   others —
16   VIVIAN: So each of the libraries carries different resources then?
17   DARREN: Well, not exactly. Over ninety percent of the books at
18   each library are the same.
19   VIVIAN: The same books!
20   DARREN: Of course.
21   VIVIAN: But wouldn't they get more accomplished if they worked
22   together and stopped duplicating each other's services?
23   DARREN: Possibly. But the librarians at the different facilities
24   rarely speak to each other, let alone work together.
25   VIVIAN: Why don't they talk to each other?
26   DARREN: You know how it is. Some are conservative librarians,
27   some literal librarians, some liberal librarians, some
28   children's librarians, and some are just content to work at the
29   reference desk. Sometimes it's pretty hard to get them to
30   agree on anything.
31   VIVIAN: Except that it's a good thing to read.
32   DARREN: Right, except for that. Say, did you want to check out a
33   book today?
34   VIVIAN: No. I, ah, well ... I don't know how to read.
35   DARREN: If you don't know how to read, why are you so

1   interested in libraries?
2 VIVIAN: For some reason I thought maybe someone here could
3   teach me. I didn't know where else to go.
4 DARREN: Yes, well, we don't have anyone on our staff who is
5   qualified to teach people to read. We specialize in medical
6   works from the eighteenth century, you know. But there is a
7   library in town for those who can't read. It's on Blakemore
8   Street, I believe. Just go down Hudson Avenue, turn right at
9   Medved and left on Washington. Follow the signs, and you
10   can't miss it.
11 VIVIAN: But I can't follow the signs. I don't know how to read
12   them!
13 DARREN: I'm sorry. Then I guess I can't help you after all.
14 VIVIAN: *(Turning to leave)* I guess not.
15 DARREN: *(After she has exited)* Next? *(Freeze. Fadeout.)*
16
17
18
19
20
21
22
23
24
25
26
27
28
29
30
31
32
33
34
35

Time-Out!

Summary: Martin is told to check into the game, but he suddenly gets cold feet.

Purpose: To show that believers are called to serve God and not just sit on the sidelines.

Time: 2-4 minutes

Tone: Lighthearted

Cast: Martin — A benchwarmer whose time has come (male); Coach — His coach who wants to put him into the game (male)

Costumes: Sweats for Coach and a basketball uniform for Martin.

Props/Set: Bench

Themes: Calling, choices, church issues, excuses, obedience, priorities, service

Text: "I know your deeds, that you are neither cold nor hot. I wish you were either one or the other! So, because you are lukewarm — neither hot nor cold — I am about to spit you out of my mouth" (Revelation 3:15-16 and Exodus 3:10-4:17 — the calling of Moses).

Notes: Use this brief sketch to get people thinking about excuses they use when God calls them to serve him. Background sounds of a basketball game are needed. You could easily change the names to make the people involved female.

1   *SETTING:* Late in a college basketball game. As the scene opens,
2   Martin is seated on the bench, bored and tuned out as usual.
3   Suddenly Coach calls a time-out and their conversation begins.
4

5   **COACH:** *(Yelling loudly, signaling to imaginary refs)* **Time-out!**
6   **Time-out!** *(Turning to the bench with imaginary players lined up,*
7   *he motions to the one on the end.)* **OK, Martin, go check in for**
8   **Harris.**
9   **MARTIN: Who, me?**
10 **COACH: Yeah, you. You're Martin, aren't you? Go check in for**
11   **Harris.**
12 **MARTIN:** *(Surprised)* **But Coach, I haven't played all year!**
13 **COACH: I know, I know, but your time has come to play. Now get**
14   **in there.**
15 **MARTIN: But Coach, uh ... I'm really not that good.**
16 **COACH: Look, you've been at practices all year. The reason we**
17   **practice is so that we're ready to play. Now get up and get in**
18   **the game.**
19 **MARTIN:** *(Standing up and pretending to favor his ankle)* **Ow!**
20   **Coach, my ankle kinda hurts. I think I should stay off it.**
21 **COACH:** *(Beginning to get angry and losing his patience)* **Baloney.**
22   **You were fine in the pre-game warmup. What's the matter**
23   **with you? Go check into the game.**
24 **MARTIN:** *(Motioning to an imaginary player on the bench)* **Coach,**
25   **maybe you should put in Lewis here. He's a better shooter**
26   **than I am, anyhow.**
27 **COACH: I'm not putting you in to shoot, I'm putting you in to play**
28   **defense!**
29 **MARTIN: But I'm really not qualified to play. I don't know**
30   **everything there is to know about basketball. Most of those**
31   **guys on the other team have been playing longer than I have!**
32   **I mean, what if they do a move I haven't seen before? And**
33   **besides, I've only known the rules for six years.**
34 **COACH: Six years is a long time to practice!**
35 **MARTIN: Listen, Coach, I don't really have time to play right now.**

1 COACH: Time to play?! What could possibly be more important
2   than the game? What do you want to do? Just sit there on the
3   bench and watch?!
4 MARTIN: Hey, now there's a good idea!
5 COACH: Look, I chose you for this team. And now I want you in
6   the game. Nobody is a benchwarmer forever on my team!
7   There comes a time to get into the game. I'd rather you played
8   for those guys *(Motioning to the other side of the court)* than
9   take up space on my bench! That kind of an attitude makes
10   me — well, it makes me sick!
11 MARTIN: You'd rather I played for the other team than keep
12   sitting on the bench?!
13 COACH: Yes!
14 MARTIN: But couldn't you put someone else in? Anyone else?
15 COACH: It's your turn to play. This is it. I want you to choose
16   right now whose team you're gonna play for. Us or them. I
17   want you off my bench!
18 MARTIN: When you say "choose now," do you mean *right* now …
19   or maybe in a little while when we're further ahead?
20 COACH: Right now!
21 MARTIN: Isn't there any chance I could think this over for a
22   while?
23 COACH: No! It's time to decide. The time-out is over. *(Freeze.*
24   *Fadeout.)*
25
26
27
28
29
30
31
32
33
34
35

The Right Medicine

Summary: Julie is concerned for Missy's health. But Missy's not worried — she's got her own system for getting healthy.

Purpose: To show that acting like a Christian doesn't make you a Christian.

Time: 5-7 minutes

Tone: Lighthearted

Cast: Missy — A sick woman ignoring her serious disease (female); Julie — Her concerned friend (female)

Props/Set: Clothes (including some workout clothes), clothes baskets, countertop

Themes: Appearances, authenticity, conversion, excuses, faith, hiding, misconceptions about Christianity, repentance, spiritual health, truth

Text: "When the Pharisees saw this, they asked his disciples, 'Why does your teacher eat with tax collectors and "sinners"?' On hearing this, Jesus said, 'It is not the healthy who need a doctor, but the sick. But go and learn what this means: "I desire mercy, not sacrifice." For I have not come to call the righteous, but sinners'" (Matthew 9:11-13).

Notes: Keep the dialog fresh and lively. Don't let Missy's illness drag the sketch down into a somber mood. Remember, she is ignoring the illness, not bothered by it.

1   ***SETTING:*** The local laundromat. Missy and Julie are folding clothes.

2

3   **JULIE: So how're you doing, Missy? Have you been feeling any**
4   **better?**
5   **MISSY:** *(Coughing)* **Oh, I'm all right.**
6   **JULIE: You don't sound very good.**
7   **MISSY: OK, to be honest, I haven't been feeling all *that* great lately.**
8   **JULIE: Well, have you been taking your medicine?**
9   **MISSY: Not exactly.**
10   **JULIE: But, Missy! Didn't the doctors say your condition can be**
11   **life-threatening?**
12   **MISSY: Well, yeah.**
13   **JULIE: Then why aren't you taking your medicine?**
14   **MISSY: I've got my own system figured out for feeling better.**
15   **JULIE: What's that?**
16   **MISSY: Well, first of all, I've been hanging around healthy people.**
17   **JULIE: What?**
18   **MISSY: You know, I've been hanging around healthy people,**
19   **hoping some of it might wear off on me.**
20   **JULIE: I don't think it works that way.**
21   **MISSY: Well, if healthy people hang around sick people, they get**
22   **sick — right?**
23   **JULIE: Well, yeah.**
24   **MISSY: There you go. *And* I've been spending one hour a week at**
25   **the fitness center.**
26   **JULIE: That's a good start.**
27   **MISSY: Of course I don't work out or anything.**
28   **JULIE: You don't?!**
29   **MISSY: No, I just watch everyone else exercise. Some of them are**
30   **really good. They work up a nice shiny sweat. Makes me tired.**
31   **JULIE: What — are you kidding me?!**
32   **MISSY: Usually I get so worn out I have to sit in the whirlpool for**
33   **fifteen minutes when they're done.**
34   **JULIE: If you're sick, watching healthy people exercise isn't going**
35   **to make you better! You need to actually exercise yourself.**

1   MISSY: Whew. That sounds like too much work to me. *(Trying to*
2   *convince JULIE she's OK)* Oh! And I've been telling everyone
3   that I'm OK.
4   JULIE: That's not gonna help you get better!
5   MISSY: Well, at least they'll think I'm healthy. And, of course, I've
6   been acting very healthy.
7   JULIE: How do you act healthy?
8   MISSY: I dress like healthy people dress. See? *(Holds up clothes she*
9   *is folding.)* I read those fitness magazines. And I learned all
10   their lingo.
11   JULIE: Whose lingo?
12   MISSY: The healthy people's.
13   JULIE: Have you been missing your appointments with the
14   therapist?
15   MISSY: *(Ignoring her)* I know all the right words! It's great. I use
16   phrases like, "Nice abs," "Cutting back on the carbs, huh?"
17   "Toss me another protein drink," and "How much can you
18   bench?" Healthy people love that kind of talk!
19   JULIE: I don't believe this!
20   MISSY: It's great!
21   JULIE: Missy, you have a life-threatening illness, and you're
22   playing games. All this stuff you're doing — attending a
23   fitness center once a week, dressing a certain way, acting like
24   someone you're not, telling healthy people you're one of them
25   and using their language — none of that's gonna make you
26   healthy!
27   MISSY: But it sure makes me feel better about myself!
28   JULIE: But you're not getting any better! You're just pretending!
29   MISSY: Then what do you suggest?
30   JULIE: You need to tackle the real problem.
31   MISSY: So what are you saying?
32   JULIE: I'm saying you need to take your medicine! I mean, you
33   can still do all that other stuff, but first take care of the
34   disease!
35   MISSY: *(Getting up to leave)* Well, if I started taking the medicine

1   and people noticed the side effects, they might figure out that
2   I've been sick this whole time. What would they think of me
3   then?
4   JULIE: That you're finally getting better?
5   MISSY: I'd rather keep things the way they are. I'm pretty popular
6   at the club, you know. *(Looking at her watch)* Oh, I gotta get
7   going. *Muscle Mountain* is on in ten minutes.
8   JULIE: Is that the show where they all lift logs out in the woods
9   wearing their bathing suits?
10   MISSY: *(Beginning to cough)* Yeah, it's really inspirational. Just
11   give me a bag of chips and a box of chocolate, and I could
12   watch it all day. I'll see ya! Thanks for the talk. I'm starting
13   to feel better already. *(Cough, cough)*
14   JULIE: But this is serious! Don't you get it?
15   MISSY: Thanks for your concern, Julie, but I'll be all right. OK?
16   I really don't feel all that bad. *(Coughing as she turns to leave)*
17   I feel fine.
18   JULIE: *(Desperately calling to her)* But Missy, wouldn't you rather
19   *become* one of the healthy people instead of just *act* like one?
20   *(Freeze. Blackout.)*
21
22
23
24
25
26
27
28
29
30
31
32
33
34
35

So You Wanna Buy a Car, Huh?

Summary: Brian wants to buy a car, but his father isn't sure he's ready yet.

Purpose: To show that what matters most about people is on the inside.

Time: 4-6 minutes

Tone: Lighthearted

Cast: Brian — A teenager obsessed with "cars" (male); Dad — His hesitant and protective father (male)

Props/Set: Car keys, lawn mower, tools in a tool box, seat belt

Themes: Appearances, dating, judging, parenting, priorities, relationships, self-control, sex, teenagers, temptation

Text: "Your beauty should not come from outward adornment, such as braided hair and the wearing of gold jewelry and fine clothes. Instead, it should be that of your inner self, the unfading beauty of a gentle and quiet spirit, which is of great worth in God's sight" (1 Peter 3:3-4).

Notes: In this sketch, choosing a car is compared to the dating process. Brian is more interested in a nice-looking model than one with quality workmanship. This sketch shows how some people value appearances over character. Have fun with the hinting and double meanings!

1 **SETTING:** The front lawn, where the lawn mower has just broken
2 down. As the scene opens, the lawn mower is On-stage. Brian
3 enters with Dad, who is carrying a toolbox.
4
5 **DAD: She broke down again, huh?**
6 **BRIAN: Yeah.**
7 **DAD: Well, let's see if I can get her running … Hmmm …** *(DAD*
8 *begins working on the mower. BRIAN stands by with his hands in*
9 *his pockets.)*
10 **BRIAN: Dad, I want to buy a car.**
11 **DAD: A car!**
12 **BRIAN: Yeah! My very own car!**
13 **DAD:** *(Nostalgically)* **Your own car, huh?** *(To BRIAN)* **I don't know**
14 **if you're old enough yet for that kind of responsibility.**
15 **BRIAN: Give me a break, Dad! I'm sixteen.**
16 **DAD: Like I just said —**
17 **BRIAN:** *(Exasperated)* **But all my friends have cars. Some have**
18 **been driving steady for months! Some of the guys in my class**
19 **have even been through a couple different models already!**
20 **DAD: But what do you know about driving a car? Who taught you**
21 **how to handle one?**
22 **BRIAN: I had this safe driving class at school. We went over all this**
23 **stuff. My teacher told us it's always safe — as long as you**
24 **wear a seat belt.**
25 **DAD: A seat belt! Is that what they're teaching you kids these**
26 **days?** *(Tips lawn mower upright.)*
27 **BRIAN: Well, yeah. They even hand 'em out for free at school.**
28 **See?** *(He pulls out a seat belt from his jacket pocket.)*
29 **DAD: I don't believe this!**
30 **BRIAN: Yeah, I mean, they know teenagers are gonna have**
31 **accidents, right? So they just give us what we need to practice**
32 **what they call "safe s-s-s-seat-belting."**
33 **DAD:** *(Holding the lawn mower and motioning with it as he talks)* **But**
34 **wouldn't it be better to teach you how to ease up on the gas,**
35 **go slow, stop pushing the limits, use caution, and when to just**

1   shut off the ignition and go for a walk?! Wouldn't that be
2   better than just *assuming* you're gonna end up in a wreck?!
3 BRIAN: *(This exchange is very quick.)* **Are you sure we're talking**
4   **about the same thing here, Dad?**
5 DAD: Cars?
6 BRIAN: Yeah.
7 DAD: Of course.
8 BRIAN: Good.
9 DAD: Why?
10 BRIAN: Never mind ... All I know is they said if you wear your seat
11   belt, you won't get hurt, even when you crash. Anyway, in the
12   locker room after gym class, the guys are always bragging
13   about their cars and how far they've gone with them! It's
14   embarrassing not having my own set of wheels!
15 DAD: Locker room talk, huh?
16 BRIAN: And I've seen a bunch of stuff on TV about driving.
17 DAD: TV shows! *(Picking up a wrench)* OK, Mr. Smarty Pants,
18   what's the most important thing to look for when you're
19   picking out a car?
20 BRIAN: Oh, that's easy. The paint job.
21 DAD: The paint job?
22 BRIAN: Yeah. That, and ... *(Really getting into this and gesturing)* if
23   it's well built and has nice curves.
24 DAD: *(Doing a double take)* **Are you sure we're talking about the**
25   **same thing here?**
26 BRIAN: *(This exchange is very quick.)* **Cars?**
27 DAD: Yeah.
28 BRIAN: Of course.
29 DAD: Good.
30 BRIAN: Why?
31 DAD: Never mind ... What about dependability? What about
32   quality? Don't you know a fancy paint job has nothing to do
33   with what a car is like on the inside? You want to get a model
34   you can rely on. One that you can trust, that'll stick with you
35   for the long haul ... unlike this lawn mower ...

1 BRIAN: Dad, no one cares about reliability! I want a car that I can
2 feel good about being seen with! One that'll impress people!
3 And the best way to do that is to get a car with a cool exterior.
4 DAD: *(Turning his attention to his son)* Listen, Brian. When I was
5 your age, I started thinking about cars, too. I started checking
6 'em out every time I saw one drive by. And my dad — your
7 grandfather — gave me some good advice.
8 BRIAN: What's that? Ride your bicycle for the rest of your life?
9 DAD: No, he just told me to be careful. "Not all cars are created
10 equal," he said. Paint jobs are nice, but it's more important to
11 know what's under the hood.
12 BRIAN: *(Sarcastically)* Brilliant advice, Dad.
13 DAD: *(Ignoring him)* Now, at first I didn't listen to him. When I
14 first went car shopping, I tried out all the cars with nice paint
15 jobs. Took them for test drives, you know?
16 BRIAN: What'd you find out?
17 DAD: Well, some were pretty nice, but lots of them were *(Banging*
18 *the lawn mower with the wrench)* clunkers. Finally I settled for
19 a model that had quality parts. Good workmanship. Long-
20 lasting value. And a pretty attractive exterior as well, I might
21 add. She was a great investment, Son! She's been reliable over
22 the years. Never let me down.
23 BRIAN: You gotta be kidding, Dad! No one keeps a car that long
24 anymore. A few months, maybe ... a couple years, then you
25 just trade it in for a newer model!
26 DAD: *(To himself)* It's sad how things have changed. *(To BRIAN)*
27 But don't you want a car that'll last a lifetime?
28 BRIAN: I'm not looking for a car I can keep forever! Just one I can
29 have fun with for a while and then get rid of.
30 DAD: But Brian —
31 BRIAN: C'mon, Dad. My own car! What do you say?
32 DAD: Be patient, Son. Your time will come ... For now, you can
33 finish mowing the lawn, and ... uh ... put that seat belt away
34 before someone sees you carrying it around. *(Pats BRIAN on*
35 *the back and smiles. They freeze. Fadeout.)*

The Intersection

Summary: Larry and Chip have arrived at an intersection. One road leads to life, the other to death. As they try to decide which road to take, they discover what they each trust most.

Purpose: To reveal that many people trust more in their common sense than in God's Word.

Time: 5-7 minutes

Tone: Lighthearted until the end

Cast: Larry — A well-meaning guy who trusts what he can see (male); Chip — His friend who wants to trust the map (male)

Costumes: Hiking gear, including boots and backpacks

Props/Set: A well-worn fold-out map, a water bottle, walking sticks

Themes: Assumptions, choices, consequences, conversion, faith, life, reality, relativism, trust, truth

Text: "Enter through the narrow gate. For wide is the gate and broad is the road that leads to destruction, and many enter through it. But small is the gate and narrow the road that leads to life, and only a few find it" (Matthew 7:13-14).

Notes: The intersection isn't real, just an imaginary space on the stage. Chip and Larry look like they've been backpacking for quite a while. Their map says they should follow one path, but their common sense tells them they should follow the other.

1   ***SETTING:*** An intersection along the road of life. As the scene opens,
2   Chip and Larry enter and cross to Center Stage.
3
4   **LARRY:** *(Taking off backpack and sighing as if he's just finished a*
5   *long hike)* **Well, here we are, huh?**
6   **CHIP: Yeah. I guess this is the intersection everyone's been telling**
7   **us about.** *(Takes off backpack and pulls out a bottle of water.)* **I**
8   **can't believe we finally made it!**
9   **LARRY: Two roads …**
10   **CHIP: That's what it looks like.**
11   **LARRY: Well … which one should we take?**
12   **CHIP: I don't know.** *(Gesturing to the right)* **This one looks pretty**
13   **well-traveled.**
14   **LARRY: It's wide and easy to follow …**
15   **CHIP: And it's downhill all the way.** *(Passes the water to LARRY.)*
16   **LARRY:** *(Taking a drink)* **Smooth sailing.**
17   **CHIP: Yeah, and** *(Gesturing to the other imaginary road)* **that one**
18   **seems rather steep and overgrown. Hmmm.**
19   **LARRY: What does the map say?**
20   **CHIP:** *(Pulling out a large topographical map and unfolding it)* **Well,**
21   **let's see. Hmmm. That's odd.**
22   **LARRY: What?**
23   **CHIP: Well, the map says one of these roads leads to life and the**
24   **other to death.**
25   **LARRY: What? I thought that was just a legend or something. Let**
26   **me see that!** *(Taking the map and reading it)* **Whoa! You're**
27   **right! Man, I don't believe it. Talk about a life-and-death**
28   **decision!**
29   **CHIP:** *(Trying to see the map)* **So which one is the life road?**
30   **LARRY: Well … this doesn't make a whole lot of sense. The map**
31   **says the road to life is the narrow, steep one, and the road**
32   **everyone seems to be choosing is the death road. Here, see for**
33   **yourself.** *(Hands CHIP the map.)*
34   **CHIP: You're right — that *doesn't* make any sense. I don't get it.**
35   **LARRY: But don't you see? It must be a mistake. People pass this**

1   way all the time, and they're all faced with the same choice —

2   which road to take. And look at which one they choose!

3 CHIP: *(Thoughtfully)* Yeah, but the map says the road to life is that

4   little pathway leading up into the forest. Something's not right

5   here.

6 LARRY: Maybe it doesn't even matter which road you take. They

7   probably both end up at the same place anyway.

8 CHIP: Not according to the map ...

9 LARRY: Well, listen. That map is pretty old and outdated, you

10   know what I mean? How do you know you can trust that thing

11   anyhow? *(Answering his own question)* You don't. Seeing is

12   believing.

13 CHIP: But which direction should we go?

14 LARRY: The way I see it, we either follow common sense or the

15   map. Either think for yourself, or let someone else do your

16   thinking for you.

17 CHIP: So you're saying?

18 LARRY: I'm saying go with your gut. Nearly everyone else who

19   walks this way chooses which road?

20 CHIP: The wide one.

21 LARRY: That's right. Now how could they all be wrong?

22 CHIP: Just because a lot of people believe something doesn't make

23   it true.

24 LARRY: Yeah, but it's a good indication! I say we take the easy

25   road.

26 CHIP: Wow. Your gut has a lot to say. My gut says trust the map.

27 LARRY: Why is that?

28 CHIP: Well, it hasn't been wrong so far.

29 LARRY: Well, I say trust what you see. And you see that forest over

30   there? *(Gesturing toward the narrow road)*

31 CHIP: Yeah?

32 LARRY: I don't trust it ... Looks pretty dark, doesn't it?

33 CHIP: Yeah.

34 LARRY: And steep?

35 CHIP: Uh-huh.

1   LARRY: And narrow.
2   CHIP: I guess so.
3   LARRY: And dangerous.
4   CHIP: OK, so what?
5   LARRY: Dark, steep, narrow, and dangerous. Does that sound like
6   the life road to you?
7   CHIP: Hmmm. I see what you mean.
8   LARRY: You wanna get all sweaty, muddy, scratched up, and
9   exhausted trudging up that trail when you can just coast
10   down this one over here? Go ahead, take a peek up that
11   narrow path. What do you see?
12 CHIP: *(Going over to the narrow road and peering up it)* Not much.
13   I can only see a few feet. There's a lot of thorns and poison ivy
14   on the trail.
15 LARRY: *(Feeling a victory coming on)* There you have it! Now take
16   a look at this path over here. No dangers. No curves. No
17   surprises. And you can see where you're going! Easy choice, if
18   you ask me.
19 CHIP: It sure does look easier … Maybe you're right.
20 LARRY: Of course I'm right! *(Picking up backpack and putting it
21   back on)* C'mon, let's get going. *(CHIP looks at the map, then at
22   LARRY, who is beginning to walk away, then back at the map.)*
23   Are you coming or what?
24 CHIP: *(Folding the map back up and stuffing it into his backpack)*
25   Yeah, yeah. I'm coming. I'm coming.
26 LARRY: Who needs a map when you've got each other? *(Slaps
27   CHIP's backpack as if he were slapping his shoulder.)* Besides,
28   I'll bet no one's taken that other trail for *years!*
29 CHIP: Yeah, you're probably right. *(Looks back over shoulder at the
30   narrow road and freezes. Fadeout.)*
31
32
33
34
35

Time to Meet

Summary: Derek is hoping to finally meet up with Jesus, but when their appointed time passes, he wonders if searching for him was really worth it.

Purpose: To show that Jesus is available to meet us each individually.

Time: 5-7 minutes

Tone: Lighthearted

Cast: Derek — A normal guy with misconceptions about Jesus (male); Stranger — Jesus incognito (male or female)

Props/Set: Jesus needs a wristwatch. Make sure Derek isn't wearing one.

Themes: Assumptions, conversion, Jesus, misconceptions about Christianity, new life, relationships, stereotypes, witnessing

Text: "Ask and it will be given to you; seek and you will find; knock and the door will be opened to you. For everyone who asks receives; he who seeks finds; and to him who knocks, the door will be opened" (Matthew 7:7-8).

Notes: Because of the nature of this sketch, Jesus could be female. Just make sure that Jesus is *not* a bearded, long-haired, hippie-looking guy. Use the actual time each time the Stranger checks his watch.

1 ***SETTING:*** A busy street corner in the middle of the city. As the scene
2   opens, Derek and Stranger are standing On-stage looking out across
3   the audience, which represents the crowd of people passing by.
4
5 **DEREK: Say, do you have the time?**
6 **STRANGER:** *(Looks at his watch and says whatever time it really is.*
7   *For example: "It's 10:59." DEREK nods his thanks.)* **Why?**
8 **DEREK: Oh, I'm supposed to be meeting someone.**
9 **STRANGER: Oh.**
10 **DEREK:** *(Looking around for a moment, scanning the crowd)* **So what**
11   **time is it now?**
12 **STRANGER: It's still _____** *(Again says the current time.)*
13 **DEREK: Are you sure?**
14 **STRANGER:** *(Checking watch again)* **Pretty sure.**
15 **DEREK:** *(Frustrated)* **Man!**
16 **STRANGER: Who are you waiting for, anyway?**
17 **DEREK: Oh, you wouldn't believe me if I told you.** *(Again scans the*
18   *crowd. This time he looks at STRANGER. STRANGER again tells*
19   *him the current time.)*
20 **STRANGER: Boy, are you anxious!**
21 **DEREK: Yeah, well, it's an important meeting.**
22 **STRANGER:** *(After a short pause)* **Listen, I'm not trying to be nosy,**
23   **but you really got my curiosity up. You got a job interview or**
24   **something?**
25 **DEREK: No.**
26 **STRANGER: Got a big date?**
27 **DEREK: No.**
28 **STRANGER: Maybe a rendezvous with a celebrity or a model or**
29   **something like that?**
30 **DEREK: No. Nothing like that.**
31 **STRANGER: Then who are you supposed to be meeting today?**
32 **DEREK:** *(Under his breath so no one can hear him; slightly*
33   *embarrassed)* **Jesus.**
34 **STRANGER: Are you kidding me?** *The* **Jesus?!**
35 **DEREK: Shhh. Keep your voice down! Yeah.** *The* **Jesus. Hey, I**

1	know it sounds crazy, but some of my friends told me if I
2	showed up here today, I could meet him.
3	**STRANGER:** That's crazy!
4	**DEREK:** I know.
5	**STRANGER:** Then why'd you come?
6	**DEREK:** I don't know. Curious, I guess.
7	**STRANGER:** *(Looking around at the crowd)* **But how are you gonna**
8	recognize him?
9	**DEREK:** What, are you kidding me? This is Jesus we're talking
10	about! How could I miss him? Everyone knows what Jesus
11	looks like!
12	**STRANGER:** They do?
13	**DEREK:** Of course!
14	**STRANGER:** Oh ... So how tall is he?
15	**DEREK:** He's ... well ... pretty tall. I guess. I mean, I don't know
16	exactly.
17	**STRANGER:** Oh. What about his hair?
18	**DEREK:** Um. Long, kinda hippie-style, I think.
19	**STRANGER:** Eye color?
20	**DEREK:** I ... um ...
21	**STRANGER:** Clothes?
22	**DEREK:** I don't know. Kind of a toga-looking thing?
23	**STRANGER:** Does he have a goatee? Mustache? Beard?
24	**DEREK:** A beard! He's got a beard, that I know! That and the long
25	hair. And he looks like this. *(DEREK poses staring into space,*
26	*holding up his hands in blessing like a stereotypical picture of*
27	*Jesus.)*
28	**STRANGER:** You sure?
29	**DEREK:** Well ... Uh ... Not really.
30	**STRANGER:** So basically you're looking for a long-haired,
31	bearded hippie wearing a toga, staring off into space?
32	**DEREK:** That's not exactly what I meant.
33	**STRANGER:** But you really don't know what he looks like?
34	**DEREK:** I guess not. What time is it now, anyway?
35	**STRANGER:** It's ... um, _____ *(Tells him the current time.)*

1   What time was Jesus supposed to show up?
2   DEREK: *(Disappointed)* Five minutes ago.
3   STRANGER: Oh, sorry.
4   DEREK: Yeah, me, too.
5   STRANGER: Really?
6   DEREK: Yeah. For what it's worth, I was really hoping to meet
7   him in person.
8   STRANGER: Why?
9   DEREK: Um ... Well, there's some stuff I was hoping to talk with
10   him about ... you know, some questions I've had ... some
11   things I was finally ready to admit to someone ... Look, I'd
12   better be going. I guess it was pretty stupid to think I'd ever
13   meet up with Jesus here today. *(Starting to leave)*
14 STRANGER: *(Nonchalantly)* People do every day.
15 DEREK: Huh? What do you mean?
16 STRANGER: Oh, I just mean people meet him every day — Jesus,
17   that is. And most of the time, he doesn't look like — or act
18   quite like — what they expect.
19 DEREK: Oh.
20 STRANGER: Anyway, it looks like you've got some time on your
21   hands. You wanna grab a cup of coffee or something?
22 DEREK: Yeah, sure, I guess ... By the way, who were you waiting
23   for?
24 STRANGER: *(They begin to exit. Lights begin to fade out.)* Oh, this
25   guy some friends of mine have been telling me about. His
26   name is Derek. They thought it was about time we met.
27 DEREK: Derek? Hey, that's my name!
28 STRANGER: Well, what a coincidence ... *(Fadeout.)*
29
30
31
32
33
34
35

Merry Wishmas!

Summary: Carter and Leah are getting ready for their favorite holiday. But do they really understand the true meaning of Wishmas?

Purpose: To reveal how distractions blur Christmas' true significance.

Time: 4-6 minutes

Tone: Lighthearted

Cast: Carter — A "normal" guy who wants to share his wish list (male); Leah — His holiday-weary wife (female)

Props/Set: Two stapled packets of printed wish lists, Christmas decorations, instrumental music

Themes: Christmas, consumerism, distractions, Jesus, misconceptions about Christianity, modern life, priorities, stereotypes

Text: "She will give birth to a son, and you are to give him the name Jesus, because he will save his people from their sins" (Matthew 1:21).

Notes: Don't print the title of this sketch in your church bulletin, or change the name to "The Holiday" so that the impact is not lost when the audience realizes the couple isn't really celebrating Christmas.

1   *SETTING:* Leah and Carter's living room, where Leah is finishing
2   putting up her Wishmas decorations. As the scene opens, Leah is
3   On-stage, decorating. She spends a few moments humming or
4   whistling the song "We Wish You a Merry Christmas" before
5   Carter enters.
6
7   CARTER: *(Entering)* **So honey, are you almost done with those**
8   **decorations?**
9   LEAH: **Just about. Here, help me with this wreath.**
10   CARTER: **I just finished writing up my wish list. Wanna hear it?**
11   LEAH: *(Reaching, putting up the wreath)* **In a minute. Oh! It's**
12   **always so much work getting ready for this holiday!**
13   CARTER: **But I thought this was one of your favorite holidays.**
14   LEAH: **Well, it is. It's just that there's so much to do! Sometimes I**
15   **almost wish it didn't even exist.**
16   CARTER: **C'mon, now, you don't mean that, do you?**
17   LEAH: **Well —**
18   CARTER: **That's not the holiday spirit! What would winter be like**
19   **without Wishmas?**
20   LEAH: **Oh, you're right — Wishmas** *is* **a great tradition, what with**
21   **wishing for all those things we really want ...**
22   CARTER: **And rushing around frantically, trying to visit all our**
23   **relatives in three days' time ...**
24   LEAH: **And eating so much that you feel guilty about it for**
25   **months ...**
26   CARTER: **And renting videos ...**
27   LEAH: **Baking cookies ...**
28   CARTER: **Getting time off work ...**
29   LEAH: **Sending out cards to people we haven't seen in years ...**
30   CARTER: **Putting up a tree ...**
31   LEAH: *(Gesturing to her handiwork)* **And decorating the house ...**
32   **Maybe you're right ...**
33   CARTER: **It just wouldn't be winter without Wishmas!** *(They finish*
34   *hanging the wreath together.)* **There ...** *(Singing)* **It's beginning**
35   **to look a lot like Wishmas!**

1   **LEAH:** *(Smiling)* **OK, now let's hear that wish list of yours …**

2   **CARTER:**   *(Reading his list)* **OK, first I'm wishing for a new**

3   **computer —**

4   **LEAH: But didn't you get a new computer last Wishmas?**

5   **CARTER: Well, yeah. But it's a year old now, isn't it?**

6   **LEAH: I guess so.**

7   **CARTER: And a new drill and a riding lawn mower and the entire**

8   *Left Behind* **series** *(Or another popular book set)* **on audio tape,**

9   **and —**

10   **LEAH:** *(Looking over his shoulder at the list)* **How many pages is**

11   **that list?**

12   **CARTER: Only sixteen.**

13   **LEAH: That's not bad. Mine's twenty.**

14   **CARTER: Well, what are some of the things on your list?**

15   **LEAH:** *(Picking her list up from the table)* **I need a bread maker and**

16   **a new mixer, a new pair of shoes —**

17   **CARTER: Shoes? Don't you have like twenty pairs of shoes**

18   **already?**

19   **LEAH: Well, yeah. But this is Wishmas, isn't it?**

20   **CARTER: You're right, dear! What else do you have on there?**

21   **LEAH: Well, you know, the usual: a new car and stereo and**

22   **bedroom set and … peace on earth.**

23   **CARTER: Peace on earth?! That's a mighty big wish, isn't it?**

24   **LEAH: Well, hey … It's Wishmas, right?**

25   **CARTER: Yeah … You know, with all the stuff going on in our**

26   **society these days, it's easy to lose sight of the real reason for**

27   **the season. We need to stay focused this year and not get so**

28   **distracted!**

29   **LEAH: Right! Even though it is a lot of work getting ready to**

30   **celebrate Wishmas, I guess it's all worth it … I mean, you**

31   **really do get a lot of new things.**

32   **CARTER: Yeah, I almost wish that Wishmas came more than once**

33   **a year!**

34   **LEAH: Maybe that's the key — making every day of the year a**

35   **little more like Wishmas.**

1 CARTER: Boy, you're right. It sure is nice recovering the true
2   meaning of Wishmas again.
3 LEAH: Yes, dear, it is … It certainly is.
4 CARTER: Well, you ready to go Wishmas caroling?
5 LEAH: *(Smiling)* Yeah.
6 CARTER and LEAH: *(Singing together as they exit arm in arm)* We
7   wish you a merry Wishmas. We wish you a merry Wishmas.
8   We wish you a merry Wishmas, and more stuff for next year!
9   *(Fadeout.)*
10
11
12
13
14
15
16
17
18
19
20
21
22
23
24
25
26
27
28
29
30
31
32
33
34
35

Light Switch

Summary: Charles and Allison have separated themselves from the evil influences of the world. But is that really the best way to keep their light burning?

Purpose: To show that Christians must stay "in the world" but not be "of the world."

Time: 4-6 minutes

Tone: Lighthearted until the end

Cast: Charles — An escapist trying to "protect his light" (male); Allison — His wife, who thinks maybe they should turn back (female)

Props/Set: Backpack, map, two pairs of sunglasses

Themes: Church issues, distractions, divisiveness, hiding, judging, life, running away, service, spiritual health

Text: "Neither do people light a lamp and put it under a bowl. Instead they put it on its stand, and it gives light to everyone in the house. In the same way, let your light shine before men, that they may see your good deeds and praise your Father in heaven" (Matthew 5:15-16).

Notes: As the sketch progresses, slowly dim the lights so that it appears to be dusk. Ambiance sounds such as howling wolves would be appropriate at the end.

1   *SETTING:* A road heading toward the mountains. Charles and Allison
2   are en route when we first meet them.
3
4   **CHARLES: Hurry up! We need to get going!**
5   **ALLISON:** *(Enters wearing a huge backpack.)* **I'm coming, I'm**
6   **coming.**
7   **CHARLES: We need to hurry.**
8   **ALLISON: I know, I know.** *(Struggling with the big pack)* **By the way,**
9   **how come I'm the one wearing this big backpack, anyhow?**
10   **CHARLES:** *(Looking at a map)* **I'm the navigator. Whew! That trail**
11   **back there sure was steep.**
12   **ALLISON: You're telling me ...**
13   **CHARLES: And that was tricky getting out of the city without**
14   **anyone seeing us! I sure am glad we made it out of there alive!**
15   **ALLISON: Me, too.**
16   **CHARLES:** *(Grabbing her arm)* **Shhh. Look up ahead ... There's**
17   **someone on the road. Quick, get down!** *(Both duck down*
18   *behind an imaginary boulder.)*
19   **ALLISON: That was close.**
20   **CHARLES: Yeah! You can't be too careful. We have to be as wise**
21   **as serpents —**
22   **ALLISON: — And as innocent as doves.**
23   **CHARLES:** *(Whispering)* **Hey, as long as we're stopped, wanna**
24   **make sure you still have it?**
25   **ALLISON: Of course I have it!**
26   **CHARLES: Can I peek?**
27   **ALLISON: Don't worry. It's in the pack.**
28   **CHARLES:** *(Peering at her backpack)* **Just a little peek. I don't see**
29   **any sign of it ...**
30   **ALLISON: It's in there. I had to cover it up back there to get**
31   **through customs. They might have been curious why we're**
32   **bringing it way out here in the mountains.**
33   **CHARLES:** *(Nodding)* **Yeah ... It's a good thing you did cover it up.**
34   **We've gotta protect that thing at all costs!**
35   **ALLISON: No kidding.**

1   CHARLES: We can't let anyone damage it or let it get dirty.

2   ALLISON: Don't worry, it's protected. I wrapped it up tightly so

3   no one will see it.

4   CHARLES: Good. *(They rise and begin their journey again.)*

5   ALLISON: So you really think this will work? Moving way out

6   here?

7   CHARLES: Of course! We're not supposed to be "of the world."

8   Some of the others had the right idea. I mean, having your

9   own radio stations and your own schools is a good start.

10 ALLISON: And bookstores.

11 CHARLES: Yeah, and restaurants, malls, and gas stations. But

12   they didn't take the idea far enough.

13 ALLISON: *(Reciting, like it's their motto)* Totally separated!

14   Protecting it at all costs! Never letting it get grimy or defiled!

15 CHARLES: You got it.

16 ALLISON: But don't you think we should share some of it?

17 CHARLES: What, are you kidding me?! And risk losing some of

18   it? Or wasting it? Or letting it get lost?

19 ALLISON: I guess you're right.

20 CHARLES: We have to be very careful about this. Remember, it's

21   like a pearl of great price. It must be protected from those who

22   would attack it or try to steal it from us.

23 ALLISON: Yeah. *(Shivering)* Brrr … It's starting to get a little

24   chilly.

25 CHARLES: Don't worry. Once we get to the mountains, we can

26   pull it out and warm up. Just don't take it out too soon, or else

27   people from the city might see it.

28 ALLISON: *(After a pause)* Charles?

29 CHARLES: Yeah?

30 ALLISON: I've been thinking … are you sure we're doing the right

31   thing?

32 CHARLES: Listen, Allison, out here in the mountains we'll finally

33   have the chance to study our Bibles all the time. And think

34   about how much time we can commit to prayer! By the way,

35   speaking of prayer, did you bring those knee pads?

1   ALLISON: Yeah, they're in the pack. *(Motioning toward her*
2   *backpack)*
3   CHARLES: Good. We'll probably need those.
4   ALLISON: But Charles, don't you think we'll get lonely out here?
5   What if it rains up in the mountains? Besides, it's starting to
6   get dark ...
7   CHARLES: Dear, that's why we have the *Light* — as a lamp to our
8   feet and a light for our path (Psalm 119:105). Trust me. This is
9   the best decision.
10   ALLISON: Yeah, I suppose you're right. No distractions out here
11   to keep us away from God. All those annoying things like
12   telemarketers ...
13   CHARLES: Beggars in the streets ...
14   ALLISON: Prisons littering the landscape ...
15   CHARLES: Crooked politicians ...
16   ALLISON: Junk mail ...
17   CHARLES: Commercials ...
18   ALLISON: Billboards ...
19   CHARLES: Movies ...
20   ALLISON: I'll bet we're the first ones ever to think of this idea!
21   CHARLES: Yeah! Cut ourselves off from all the evil influences of
22   the world, and we'll be able to serve God wholeheartedly and
23   let his light shine bright! What do you say, shall we have a
24   little peek at that Light?
25   ALLISON: *(Taking off the backpack)* Oh, all right.
26   CHARLES: Put on your sunglasses! *(They each pull out sunglasses*
27   *and open the backpack as stage lights continue to fade out.)* Are
28   you sure you packed it?
29   ALLISON: Yeah! The Light was in there when we left.
30   CHARLES: Then where is it? How come it's not in here now?
31   ALLISON: I don't know. Are you sure it's not there?
32   CHARLES: There is no light in this bag!
33   ALLISON: Maybe it went out.
34   CHARLES: It went out? Oh, no! It's not supposed to go out! How
35   could it go out?

1   **ALLISON: You mean we're stuck way out here in the middle of**
2   **nowhere without any light? What are we gonna do?**
3   **CHARLES: I don't know.**
4   **ALLISON:** *(Silence as the lights dim even more)* **Charles?**
5   **CHARLES: Yeah, Leah?**
6   **ALLISON: I'm getting cold.**
7   **CHARLES: Me too ... Me too ...** *(They freeze. Play the sound of*
8   *wolves howling. Blackout.)*
9
10
11
12
13
14
15
16
17
18
19
20
21
22
23
24
25
26
27
28
29
30
31
32
33
34
35

Part 4
Biblical
Sketches

Have you ever tried to tell a joke to someone who's heard it before? Unless you tell it in a different way or from a different perspective, they'll probably lose interest — or even worse, beat you to the punch line.

Many people, even if they haven't grown up "in the church," are familiar with Bible stories such as Noah's ark, the Ten Commandments, and Moses parting the Red Sea. When a message is focused on one of these familiar stories, people can tune out as they jump ahead to the punch line.

"Oh, I've heard that one already. I know how it ends."

The Bible stories and readings in this section are presented in fresh and creative ways to get people thinking about what the Bible really says and how it might apply to their lives today.

Crossing the Sea

Summary: Rebekah becomes distracted while crossing the Red Sea. She convinces Josiah to stay with her rather than continue his journey.

Purpose: To show that following God means following him all the way, not just while it's convenient or interesting.

Time: 4-6 minutes

Tone: Lighthearted until the end

Cast: Josiah — An excited Israelite crossing the Red Sea (male); Rebekah — His tired and easily distracted wife (female)

Costumes: Biblical robes

Props/Set: Lots of shells, stones, starfish, etc.

Themes: Choices, consequences, distractions, frustration, obedience, patience, priorities, temptation, trust

Text: "Then he called the crowd to him along with his disciples and said: 'If anyone would come after me, he must deny himself and take up his cross and follow me'" (Mark 8:34).

Notes: This retelling of the episode of the Israelites crossing the Red Sea shows what might have happened if a couple decided not to cross all the way. Use ambiance sounds of horses and chariots and wind and waves if you desire.

1 *SETTING:* Halfway across the Red Sea. As the scene opens, they enter,
2   pretending to be on the path through the sea. Josiah is in awe of
3   the miracle. Rebekah is distracted by the pretty shells.
4
5 **JOSIAH: Can you believe this, Rebekah? The Red Sea! I mean, we**
6   **are halfway across the *Red Sea*!**
7 **REBEKAH:** *(Not paying attention to him, staring at her feet where*
8   *there are shells and stones scattered)* **Wow! This is great!**
9 **JOSIAH: I'll say! The *Red Sea!* Well, this looks like as good a place**
10   **as any for a breather. Take a load off, you know what I mean?**
11 **REBEKAH:** *(Poking around at the floor)* **These sure are cool shells,**
12   **Josiah!**
13 **JOSIAH: I thought for sure we were goners back there when the**
14   **Egyptians showed up. I mean, chariots! And horses! And**
15   **soldiers — the whole shebang!**
16 **REBEKAH: Look at this! A sand dollar!**
17 **JOSIAH: And then whamo-slamo-kablamo! Back go the waves, up**
18   **goes the water. Whoosh! Now feel that.** *(He stomps on the*
19   *ground.)* **This ground is packed as hard as those bricks we used**
20   **to make for the Egyptians. And look at this.** *(Mimes feeling*
21   *along a wall of water.)* **The water is standing straight up!**
22 **REBEKAH:** *(Looking up long enough to watch him)* **You know, if**
23   **there wasn't any water there, you'd look like a mime.**
24 **JOSIAH: A mime? What's that?**
25 **REBEKAH: Oh, never mind. There sure is a gold mine of shells**
26   **here!**
27 **JOSIAH: Is that all you've been doing? Looking at shells?**
28 **REBEKAH: They're beautiful!**
29 **JOSIAH: Sure, but —**
30 **REBEKAH:** *(Looking at the water)* **Whoa! What was that? A fish**
31   **just swam by! Did you see that? Walls of water ... I'll bet**
32   **people would pay big money to see something like this — to**
33   **walk through a path of dry land and watch fish swim by on**
34   **both sides. Hmmm ... But what would you call it?**
35 **JOSIAH: C'mon, Rebekah, look back there. I see some dust. I**

1   think Pharaoh's army is following us across! We'd better get
2   going.
3   REBEKAH: I wanna stay here.
4   JOSIAH: What?
5   REBEKAH: I like it here.
6   JOSIAH: But we're not across the sea yet!
7   REBEKAH: I know, but it's such a long walk.
8   JOSIAH: A long walk! But we can't stop in the middle. We need to
9   go all the way across. It's the only way!
10   REBEKAH: Says who?
11   JOSIAH: Says ... God!
12   REBEKAH: Well, I'm tired of doing things God's way all the time.
13   Plagues of flies and hail and frogs — I really hated those frogs.
14   And then that whole lamb-killing-blood-on-the-doorframe
15   thing — that was just plain disgusting. And now this ...
16   deserts and walking through the sea. Following this God of
17   Moses is dangerous!
18   JOSIAH: It's exciting!
19   REBEKAH: But things were easier back in Egypt. And safer!
20   JOSIAH: Faith is always dangerous —
21   REBEKAH: And more predictable. Everything was fine until
22   Moses and his God had to come along.
23   JOSIAH: We were slaves!
24   REBEKAH: Yeah, but at least we had someone to take care of us.
25   JOSIAH: C'mon, God is taking care of us! Don't you think it's at
26   least a little bit exciting having God lead us each day?
27   REBEKAH: It's not really my thing. I'd rather know what I'm up
28   against.
29   JOSIAH: But God is on our side!
30   REBEKAH: I'm more into security.
31   JOSIAH: Look around you! Don't you think a God who can do this
32   *(Miming the wall of water again)* is able to keep you safe? I
33   mean, this *(Pounding the ground with his foot again)* is security.
34   REBEKAH: Maybe for you. For me, it's exhausting. And besides,
35   I just got comfortable here. And there's so much to look at ...

1   You can go on if you like. I'm gonna stay here for a while. *(Sits*

2   *down cross-legged and begins to play with the shells.)*

3   JOSIAH: *(Hesitating, unsure what to do)* OK. I'll stay for a few

4   minutes.

5   REBEKAH: Good. You can help me build a sand castle.

6   JOSIAH: *(He sits and they mime building a sand castle. Suddenly*

7   *JOSIAH looks around.)* Um, you notice anything strange?

8   REBEKAH: *(Sarcastically)* You mean besides those walls of water

9   and the fish swimming by?

10 JOSIAH: The ground ... It doesn't seem as hard as it did a minute

11   ago. Um ... It's kind of damp ...

12 REBEKAH: *(Distracted)* Oh goody — look, a starfish!

13 JOSIAH: Do you hear those chariots? Look! See those horses?

14 REBEKAH: *(Excitedly)* Seahorses? Where?

15 JOSIAH: I don't like this ... The sand is really getting moist.

16   C'mon, Rebekah, let's get going!

17 REBEKAH: *(Still distracted)* In a minute, in a minute —

18 JOSIAH: That's it! I'm getting out of here! *(JOSIAH exits.)*

19 REBEKAH: *(Whistling and playing for a few more moments, she*

20   *holds a shell up to her ear and calls for JOSIAH.)* This is

21   amazing! Josiah, listen to this! It's almost like you can hear

22   the ocean in this — Josiah? Josiah? Hello? Anybody? *(Stands,*

23   *looks to the water on the left then on the right, then looks to the*

24   *audience.)* Josiah? Uh-oh ... Um, maybe stopping in the

25   middle wasn't such a good idea after all ... *(She brings her*

26   *hand up to her face and bites her fingers in a frightened pose and*

27   *freezes. If desired, add a moment of ambiance sound of water*

28   *rushing in, then blackout.)*

29

30

31

32

33

34

35

Chariots of Fire

Summary: God has just miraculously rescued the Israelites. A reporter is interviewing one of the eyewitnesses.

Purpose: To reveal that we need not fear when God is on our side.

Time: 4-6 minutes

Tone: Lighthearted

Cast: Terry — A movie critic-turned-television reporter (male or female); Servant — The servant of Elisha, God's prophet (male)

Costumes: A contemporary suit for Terry and biblical garb for the Servant

Props/Set: Hand-held microphone for Terry

Themes: Faith, God's power, questions, trust

Text: "What, then, shall we say in response to this? If God is for us, who can be against us?" (Romans 8:31).

Notes: If there are popular movie titles in your region, insert them into the script where appropriate. Make sure whomever you cast for Terry is a little bit goofy. God delivered the Israelites from danger. He can still deliver people from difficult circumstances today.

1   ***SETTING:*** A deserted road in ancient Israel. As the scene opens, Terry
2   is On-stage, holding the microphone. He is dressed like a
3   newscaster. Servant is dressed in biblical attire.
4
5   **TERRY: Terry Picklewickle here — movie critic for Channel Six**
6   **News. I'm filling in for Cameron Roberts, who's on**
7   **assignment. I'm on the scene in Samaria, where the King of**
8   **Israel has just thrown a party for the troops of Aram. Yes, let**
9   **me repeat that: Even though they're at war with each other as**
10   **we speak, the King of Israel has just thrown a party for the**
11   **Aramean army. This is incredible late-breaking news —**
12   *(Turning to SERVANT, who is rushing across the stage)* **Sir! Sir,**
13   **were you at the party? Did you witness these strange events?**
14   **SERVANT: Witness them? I almost caused the whole thing!**
15   **TERRY: Witness? Did you say *Witness*? Wait a minute. Are you**
16   **Harrison Ford?**
17   **SERVANT: No, I'm the servant of Elisha, the prophet of God.**
18   **TERRY: Prophet of God?**
19   **SERVANT: Yes! You should have been there —**
20   **TERRY: Where?**
21   **SERVANT: Back in Dothan.**
22   **TERRY: Gotham? Like in *Batman*?**
23   **SERVANT: No, Dothan, like in Israel. I got up early to go for a walk**
24   **outside the city, and I saw the troops — hundreds, no,**
25   ***thousands*** **of them, along with horses and chariots,**
26   **surrounding our city! I ran back to tell Elisha. "What are we**
27   **gonna do?" I asked. Then he said, "Don't be afraid. Those**
28   **who are with us are more than those who are with them"** (2
29   Kings 6:16). **I couldn't believe him! "Hello! Earth to Elisha!**
30   **Are you crazy? We are in Dothan! We have a couple of**
31   **farmers, a few steak knives, and a donkey. We're no match for**
32   **an Aramean raiding party!"**
33   **TERRY: Raiding party? Like in *Raiders of the Lost Ark*? So then**
34   **what? Did the Nazis attack?**
35   **SERVANT: Not Nazis! Arameans! And no, they didn't have time to.**

1   Elisha prayed, and then — you're not going to believe this.
2   TERRY: Try me.
3   SERVANT: OK. After he prayed, I looked out and I saw an even
4   bigger army —
5   TERRY: More Nazis? Russians? Iraqi soldiers?!
6   SERVANT: No! This was an army with horses and chariots of fire!
7   TERRY: *Chariots of Fire?* That won an Oscar!
8   SERVANT: This was no movie. These were angels!
9   TERRY: *Angels in the Outfield? A City of Angels?* What then? Were
10   you *Touched by an Angel?* Did they attack the Nazis?
11   SERVANT: Arameans! And no, they didn't have to. Then Elisha
12   prayed again.
13   TERRY: For a better script?
14   SERVANT: There was no movie! Elisha asked God to make the
15   Arameans blind. All of a sudden they started tripping and
16   stumbling around and running into each other.
17   TERRY: What about the guys with the *Chariots of Fire* chasing the
18   *Raiders of the Lost Ark* through Gotham trying to catch the
19   *Angels in the Outfield*? Were they upset because they were
20   missing the movie?
21   SERVANT: *There was no movie!* The chariots of fire weren't even
22   needed. God showed them to me because I was afraid. Elisha
23   just smirked and said, "Watch this." Then he went up to the
24   soldiers and said, "Hey, you guys! I know who you're looking
25   for, but this is the wrong city. Take my hand and follow me,
26   and I'll take you to him." But the whole time it was Elisha
27   they were looking for!
28   TERRY: Are you sure this wasn't Gotham? That sounds like
29   something the Riddler would do —
30   SERVANT: *Listen to me. Movies haven't even been invented yet!* So
31   anyway, the Arameans held hands, and Elisha led them all the
32   way to Samaria. He told the king not to kill them, but to treat
33   them like his guests rather than his enemies, like his friends
34   rather than his foes. And that's the whole story. The king
35   threw a party and then let them go! I don't think they'll be

197

1   bothering us again anytime soon.

2   **TERRY:** Amazing. Unbelievable. I'd give Elisha two thumbs up for

3   his performance in this epic drama.

4   **SERVANT:** Hey, give credit where credit is due.

5   **TERRY:** To you? To Elisha's agent? To the producer?

6   **SERVANT:** No, to the director — God. If it hadn't been for him, we

7   would have been goners for sure back there in Gotham. Wait,

8   Dothan. Now you've got me doing it! See you later! I gotta get

9   going and spread the news! *(Hurrying Off-stage)*

10   **TERRY:** *(To audience)* Well, there you have it, folks. God gets the

11   credit for this blockbuster production. Remember his chariots

12   of fire the next time you feel trapped and outnumbered. If

13   God can turn a war between Israel and Aram into a party, he

14   can turn your problems around as well. This is Terry

15   Picklewickle, signing off. *(As he exits)* Anybody got any

16   popcorn? *(Fadeout.)*

17

18

19

20

21

22

23

24

25

26

27

28

29

30

31

32

33

34

35

Something to Do

Summary: Dave has everything that a man could want. But now that he has some extra time on his hands, he notices a beautiful woman taking a bath, and one thing leads to another.

Purpose: To show that temptation and idleness go hand in hand.

Time: 4-6 minutes

Tone: Serious

Cast: Dave — A bored and susceptible king (male); Servant — His faithful and obedient servant (male)

Costumes: Either biblical or contemporary clothing with a wealthy appearance for Dave and a plainer look for the servant

Props/Set: A lounge chair or recliner

Themes: Adultery, boredom, distractions, excuses, lust, obedience, purity, rest, self-control, sex, temptation

Text: 2 Samuel 11-12 and "Have mercy on me, O God, according to your unfailing love; according to your great compassion blot out my transgressions. Wash away all my iniquity and cleanse me from my sin" (Psalm 51:1-2).

Notes: You could have a female actor enter at the end of the sketch to walk Off-stage with Dave, arm in arm.

1 **SETTING:** Dave's palace. As the scene opens, Dave is seated On-
2 stage, staring off into space or up at the ceiling.
3
4 DAVE: **Finally! Spring is here! It sure has been a long winter —**
5 **long and cold. What a winter. Time to get out and enjoy the**
6 **warm, dry weather again. Maybe I'll even head out to the**
7 **mountains like I used to — yeah, in the good ole days, hiking**
8 **in the mountains. Before all of this ...** *(Sweeping hand in large*
9 *arcing motion)*
10 **The good ole days. I never would have thought I'd end up**
11 **in a palace. I always thought I'd end up being a farmer or a**
12 **shepherd for the rest of my life. Or maybe a soldier. How I**
13 **dreamed of being a soldier! Or maybe a musician. I used to**
14 **sing all the time ...** *(Standing now and beginning to pace)*
15 **I am so bored! There's got to be something to do! Maybe I**
16 **should go and play with the kids, or take a walk with my**
17 **wife ... maybe I should, but maybe I don't want to! It's been**
18 **a long winter, and I need a break! Some time to myself! I**
19 **deserve it. Maybe I'll just sit here and take in the view. This**
20 **spring was supposed to be my vacation. God knows I've**
21 **earned it. The last few years have been** *(Here he pauses and*
22 *utters the next word slowly, with his eyes transfixed on something*
23 *in the distance that the audience cannot see)* **un-be-liev-able.**
24 *(Quickly turning away, he changes the subject.)* **Unbelievable. I**
25 **know it's warm, but sunbathing in that?** *(Turns away and paces*
26 *again.)*
27 **Maybe I should spend some time reading. That's a good**
28 **idea. Reading. Some of the old books. Or I could have them**
29 **read to me. Maybe that's what I'll do tonight. Immerse myself**
30 **in a good book.** *(Looking again at the sight in the distance. It's*
31 *beginning to be clear that he is struggling with trying to convince*
32 *himself to look away, but he is losing.)* **Dave, get ahold of**
33 **yourself! You know you shouldn't be watching this, you're a**
34 **married man!** *(Turning away again)*
35 **I wonder how the campaign is going. I haven't heard any**

1 news from the front in weeks. Sometimes I almost feel like I
2 should be with them ... No! I'm on vacation! I've earned this.
3 I did my time as a soldier. I've proven myself. I sure hope
4 we're not losing the battle ... *(Looking up again slowly)* Whoa.
5 I wonder who she is? I know I've seen her around here
6 before ... Can't place her ... She sure is beautiful ... *(Looking*
7 *away abruptly)*
8   *(To himself)* Dave, what are you doing? You shouldn't be
9 staring like that! Still, there's nothing wrong with just
10 glancing out at the landscape, is there? After all, I'm enjoying
11 the view, so to speak. I mean, I can't help it if she decided
12 to ... *(Looking back at her)* It's not like I was looking for
13 trouble.
14   *(DAVE claps his hands twice and his SERVANT appears.*
15 *Without even turning to look at him, DAVE speaks:)* Look. Do
16 you see that woman? She's beautiful. Find out who she is.
17 SERVANT: Sir, you already know her. That's the wife of one of
18 your bodyguards. She has dined here in the palace before. Her
19 name is —
20 DAVE: Ah, yes. I remember her now. Send for her.
21 SERVANT: But sir —
22 DAVE: Send for her!
23 SERVANT: Yes, sir. *(SERVANT exits.)*
24 DAVE: *(Rationalizing)* Yes, this'll be fine. It'll be nice to have some
25 company tonight. We'll dine, and then I'll send her on her
26 way. A quick meal, a little conversation. Surely there's nothing
27 wrong with having a meal together. A meal with a friend of the
28 family. Someone to talk with, something to do. When the war
29 is over, her husband will probably thank me for showing this
30 kindness to her while he was away. That's all this is — a
31 chance to help out a friend. Surely there's nothing wrong with
32 that!
33 SERVANT: *(Entering)* Sir, she's here.
34 DAVE: Send her in.
35 SERVANT: *(Apprehensively)* Sir, what shall I say to your wife?

1   **DAVE:**   Say I have business to attend to this evening!
2   **SERVANT:**   Yes, sir.
3   **DAVE:**   *(Turning to an unseen woman Off-stage. DAVE looks at her for*
4   *a long moment before speaking.)* **Hello. What was your name**
5   **again? Bathsheba … Yes … That's a beautiful name. Thank**
6   **you for accepting my invitation, Bathsheba. Come. Tonight,**
7   **we dine together …** *(Exit. Fadeout.)*
8
9
10
11
12
13
14
15
16
17
18
19
20
21
22
23
24
25
26
27
28
29
30
31
32
33
34
35

Bellyaching

Summary: When Jonah refused to obey God, he became fish food. Now that he's had some time to think things over, he's ready to do what God says. But is it too late?

Purpose: To demonstrate that repentance requires a genuine change of heart.

Time: 3-5 minutes

Tone: Lighthearted

Cast: Jonah — A reluctant servant of God (male); Stagehand — (male or female)

Costume: Biblical robe

Props/Set: Four placards with the following lettered on: 1. Day 1, 2. Day 2, 3. Day 3, 4. The Beach Just Outside Nineveh

Themes: Authenticity, calling, choices, evangelism, God's power, grace, missions, obedience, prayer, regrets, repentance, running away, second chances

Text: "From inside the fish Jonah prayed to the Lord his God. 'In my distress I called to the Lord, and he answered me. From the depths of the grave I called for help, and you listened to my cry'" (Jonah 2:1-2).

Notes: Only one person is involved in this sketch, but a second person is needed to carry the placards across the stage.

1   ***SETTING:*** Inside the giant fish's tummy. As the scene opens, Jonah is
2   seated Center Stage, scrunched up small in a ball. Stagehand
3   crosses the stage carrying a large placard that reads "Day 1.")
4
5   **JONAH:** *(To himself)* **OK ... So ... Here I am. Not much room to**
6   **move around. Not much room to do anything. Stuck in the**
7   **belly of a fish. Who'd ever believe it?** *(To God)* **All right, God!**
8   **I get the idea! You have my attention! You're not happy with**
9   **me running away. Got it. You can let me out now! No, wait a**
10   **minute, I didn't mean that. I'm probably a thousand feet**
11   **underwater by now. Don't let me out right here. Take me back**
12   **to the ship, and I promise I'll go to Nineveh ... Did you hear**
13   **me? I promise to go to Nineveh this time! We can start over**
14   **and forget this whole thing ever happened. OK? God? Are**
15   **you there?**
16   *(STAGEHAND walks by with another placard reading "Day 2."*
17   *JONAH continues speaking to God.)* **I guess the ship idea is out**
18   **of the question by now ... Hey, by the way — that storm back**
19   **there — that was a nice touch. I sure didn't expect a fish to be**
20   **my lifeboat. I thought for sure you wanted me dead. I didn't**
21   **expect another chance. I'm, uh, well, I'm sorry, God. Can you**
22   **hear me? Where are we going? Back home, so I can start over**
23   **again? Back to the shipyard? God, I'm sorry about running**
24   **away. I mean it this time. Are you up there? Can you hear me?**
25   *(STAGEHAND walks by again with the "Day 3" sign. JONAH*
26   *talks to himself.)* **It's really hot in here. No, wait, it's not the**
27   **heat, it's the humidity ... And the smell ... Whew! I'll never**
28   **eat fish again, that's for sure. I'll bet I smell like fish guts when**
29   **I get out ... If I get out ... I sure don't deserve to get out. I**
30   **really let God down. I knew what he wanted me to do, and I**
31   **ran in the exact opposite direction. I suppose he's probably**
32   **gonna let me die down here. That's what I deserve ...** *(To God)*
33   **Hey God, if you decide to let me die down here, that's OK.**
34   **Thanks for keeping me alive for a few days so I could realize**
35   **it was my fault and not yours. I should have done what you**

1   wanted. I know that now, God ... I know that now.

2   *(This time the placard the STAGEHAND carries reads "The*
3   *Beach Just Outside Nineveh." JONAH stands up and looks*
4   *around during this last section, turning to a group of imaginary*
5   *bystanders or addressing the audience.)* Wow! I can't believe it!
6   He let me out! He really did! Hey, you guys, listen! God just
7   let me out of a giant fish! No, I haven't been out in the sun too
8   long ... By the way, what town is that over there? Nineveh?
9   Cool! Hey listen, God really loves you guys — believe me, *does*
10   *he ever love you guys*! Listen, he's ready to forgive you. It
11   doesn't matter what you've done! I mean, just look at me!
12   Well, actually, don't look at me, I'm covered with fish vomit.
13   Look to him! I ran away from him, and he still loves me! He
14   gave me a second chance! And you get one, too! C'mon. Have
15   I got a story to tell you! *(Freeze. Blackout.)*

16
17
18
19
20
21
22
23
24
25
26
27
28
29
30
31
32
33
34
35

The Passover Lamb

Summary: In this sketch, listeners glimpse the true Passover Lamb from three different perspectives.

Purpose: To show that all of Scripture's promises were fulfilled in Christ.

Time: 5-7 minutes

Tone: Worshipful

Cast: Teller #1 — (male or female); Teller #2 — (male or female)

Props/Set: None

Themes: Easter, forgiveness, Jesus, new life, Passover, promises, prophecy fulfillment

Text: Various

Notes: This dramatic presentation of Scripture involves two storytellers. Begin with one storyteller at Stage Right, the other at Stage Left. After each teller says her part, she steps toward Center Stage. They should arrive at Center Stage immediately before the part where they say, "So they prepared the Passover." This movement toward Center Stage symbolizes the coming together of the Old and New Testaments in Christ — the Passover Lamb, whose blood brought freedom, forgiveness, and deliverance. Note the similarity between the consecutive readings. Have your actors emphasize the common words or ideas.

1   *(TELLER #1 and TELLER #2 are in place, one at either side of*
2   *the stage.)*
3   **TELLER #1: Moses and Aaron performed all these wonders before**
4   **Pharaoh, but the Lord hardened Pharaoh's heart, and he**
5   **would not let the Israelites go out of his country** (Exodus
6   11:10). *(Steps toward Center Stage and then scans the audience*
7   *— rather than freezing — while TELLER #2 says her part. Repeat*
8   *this procedure each time.)*
9   **TELLER #2: But when the time had fully come, God sent his Son,**
10   **born of a woman, born under the law, to redeem those under**
11   **the law ...** (Galatians 4:4-5a). *(Steps toward Center Stage, scans,*
12   *etc.)*
13   **TELLER #1: And the Lord said to Moses and Aaron, "Tell the**
14   **whole community of Israel that on the tenth day of this**
15   **month, each man is to take a lamb for his family, one for each**
16   **household ... "** (Exodus 12:1, 3).
17   **TELLER #2: In those days John the Baptist came, preaching in the**
18   **Desert of Judea. One day John saw Jesus coming toward him**
19   **and said, "Behold! The Lamb of God, who takes away the sin**
20   **of the world!"** (Matthew 3:1, John 1:29).
21   **TELLER #1:** *(The next two exchanges are quicker, almost interrupting*
22   *each other.)* **Take care of them until the fourteenth day of the**
23   **month ...** (Exodus 12:6a).
24   **TELLER #2: From that time on, Jesus began to explain to his**
25   **disciples that he must go to Jerusalem and suffer many**
26   **things ...** (Matthew 16:21a).
27   **TELLER #1: ... When all the people of the community of Israel**
28   **must slaughter them at twilight"** (Exodus 12:6b).
29   **TELLER #2: ... And that he must be killed** (Matthew 16:21).
30   **TELLER #1:** *(Pause for a beat)* **"The blood will be a sign for you on**
31   **the houses where you are: and when I see the blood, I will pass**
32   **over you. No destructive plague will strike you when I strike**
33   **Egypt. This is the Lord's Passover"** (Exodus 12:13).
34   **TELLER #2: Then came the day of Unleavened Bread on which**
35   **the Passover lamb had to be sacrificed. Jesus knew that the**

1   time had come for him to leave this world and go to the

2   **Father ...** (Luke 22:7, John 13:1).

3   **TELLER #1: Then Moses summoned all the elders of Israel and**

4   **said to them, "Go at once and select the animals for your**

5   **families and slaughter the Passover Lamb"** (Exodus 12:21).

6   **TELLER #2: He sent Peter and John, saying, "Go and make**

7   **preparations for us to eat the Passover"** (Luke 22:8).

8   **TELLER #1: The Israelites did just what the Lord commanded**

9   **Moses and Aaron ...** (Exodus 12:50).

10   **TELLER #2: They left and found things just as Jesus had told**

11   **them. So they prepared the Passover** (Luke 22:13).

12   **TELLER #1: ... So they prepared the Passover.** *(After pausing a*

13   *beat, TELLER #1 continues by sharing the verses from the*

14   *Revelation of St. John. If you desire, this could be a third teller*

15   *who begins the sketch standing motionless at Center Stage.*

16   *TELLER #2's part would remain the same.)* **Then I saw a Lamb,**

17   **looking like it had been slain, standing in the center of the**

18   **throne, encircled by the four living creatures and the elders**

19   (Revelation 5:6).

20   **TELLER #2: After supper, when they had sung a hymn, they went**

21   **out to the Mount of Olives ...** (Matthew 26:30).

22   **TELLER #1: And they sang a new song: "You are worthy to take**

23   **the scroll and to open its seals, because you were slain ... "**

24   (Revelation 5:9a).

25   **TELLER #2: Then Pilate released Barabbas to them. But Jesus he**

26   **had flogged, and handed him over to be crucified** (Mark

27   15:15).

28   **TELLER #1: " ... And with your blood you purchased men for God**

29   **from every tribe and nation!"** (Revelation 5:96).

30   **TELLER #2: So they crucified him, and with him two others — one**

31   **on each side and Jesus in the middle. About the ninth hour**

32   **Jesus cried out in a loud voice, "My God, my God! Why have**

33   **you forsaken me?" Later, Jesus said, "It is finished." With**

34   **that, he bowed his head and gave up his spirit** (John 19:18,

35   Matthew 27:46, John 19:30).

1   **TELLER #1:** *(With energy, building to a crescendo)* **Then I heard**
2   **every creature in heaven and on earth and under the earth**
3   **and on the sea, and all that is in them singing: "To him who**
4   **sits on the throne and to the Lamb be praise and honor and**
5   **glory and power forever and ever!"** (Revelation 5:13).
6   **TELLER #2: Behold! The Lamb of God, who takes away the sin of**
7   **the world!** (John 1:29).
8   **TELLER #1: The blood will be a sign for you. When I see the**
9   **blood, I will pass over you** (Exodus 12:13). *(You may wish to*
10   *have the actors say this last part in unison, raising their hands as*
11   *they say "Amen!" and then bowing down in worship.)*
12   **TOGETHER: The four living creatures said, "Amen!" and the**
13   **elders fell down and worshiped** (Revelation 5:14). *(Freeze and*
14   *blackout, or immediately transition to upbeat worship music.)*

The Story of Life

Summary: Two storytellers recite Scripture references to prophecies about the Messiah, and the fulfillment of those prophecies in Jesus of Nazareth.

Purpose: To show how Christ fulfilled the Old Testament messianic prophecies.

Time: 5-7 minutes

Tone: Worshipful

Cast: Teller #1 — (male or female); Teller #2 — (male or female)

Props/Set: None

Themes: Easter, forgiveness, Jesus, new life, promises, prophecy fulfillment

Text: Various, and "For no matter how many promises God has made, they are 'Yes' in Christ. And so through him the 'Amen' is spoken by us to the glory of God" (2 Corinthians 1:20).

Notes: Here is another dramatic presentation of Scripture's promises regarding Jesus Christ. Begin with one storyteller at Stage Right, the other at Stage Left. While one teller is reciting her part, the other scans the audience rather than freezing. (The Scripture is taken from the New International Version, with a few wording changes for readability.)

1   *(TELLER #1 and TELLER #2 are in place, one at either side of*
2   *the stage.)*
3   TELLER #1: Oh this is a wondrous story!
4   TELLER #2: And I have a story to tell ...
5   TELLER #1: It's a story you've heard ...
6   TELLER #2: It's a story you know ...
7   TELLER #1: This is the story of ...
8   TELLER #2: Life!
9   TELLER #1: The Old Testament prophets spoke of the One to
10   come ...
11   TELLER #2: The New Testament writers wrote of the One who
12   came ...
13   TELLER #1: And the prophet spoke and said, "The virgin will be
14   with child and will give birth to a son, and you will call him
15   Immanuel, which means, 'God with us'" (Isaiah 7:14).
16   TELLER #2: Ah! And the angel said to her, "Do not be afraid,
17   Mary, you have found favor with God. You will be with child
18   and give birth to a son, and you are to give him the name
19   Jesus" ... "How can this be," Mary asked, "since I am a
20   virgin?" The angel answered, "The Holy Spirit will come upon
21   you ... Nothing is impossible with God" (Luke 1:30, 34, 35, 37).
22   TELLER #1: Seven hundred years before his birth, it was Micah
23   who wrote, "But you, Bethlehem Ephrathah, though you are
24   small among the clans of Judah, out of you will come for me
25   one who will be ruler over Israel, whose origins are from of
26   old, from ancient times" (Micah 5:2).
27   TELLER #2: While they were in Bethlehem, the time came for the
28   baby to be born, and she gave birth to her firstborn, a son
29   (Luke 2:6).
30   TELLER #1: He grew up before him like a tender shoot, and like
31   a root out of dry ground (Isaiah 53:2).
32   TELLER #2: And Jesus grew in wisdom and stature, and in favor
33   with God and men (Luke 2:52).
34   TELLER #1: Moses said, "The Lord your God will raise up for you
35   a prophet like me from among your own brothers. You must

1   listen to him!" (Deuteronomy 18:15).

2   **TELLER #2: Yes! And on the last and greatest day of the Feast,**
3   **Jesus stood up and taught the people ... On hearing his words,**
4   **some of the people said, "Surely this man is the Prophet!"**
5   (John 7:40).

6   **TELLER #1: Not only the prophet, but the king! Zechariah wrote,**
7   **"Rejoice, O Daughter of Zion! Shout, Daughter of Jerusalem!**
8   **See, your king comes to you, righteous and having salvation,**
9   **gentle and riding on a donkey"** (Zechariah 9:9).

10   **TELLER #2: They brought the donkey and the colt; placed their**
11   **cloaks on them and Jesus sat on them ... When Jesus entered**
12   **Jerusalem, the whole city was stirred and asked, "Who is**
13   **this?"** (Matthew 21:7-10).

14   **TELLER #1:** *(With feeling)* **Who is this? This is the one who forgives**
15   **sins! For Jeremiah wrote, "'This is the covenant I will make**
16   **with the house of Israel after that time,' declares the Lord. 'I**
17   **will put my law in their minds and write it on their hearts. I**
18   **will be their God and they will be my people. For I will forgive**
19   **their wickedness and will remember their sins no more'"**
20   (Jeremiah 31:31-34).

21   **TELLER #2: Then he took the cup, gave thanks, and offered it to**
22   **them, saying, "This cup is the new covenant in my blood,**
23   **which is poured out for many for the forgiveness of sins"**
24   (Matthew 26:27-28, Luke 22:20).

25   **TELLER #1:** *(Slowly, sadder)* **Yet Isaiah wrote, "He was despised**
26   **and rejected by men, a man of sorrows, and familiar with**
27   **suffering"** (Isaiah 53:3).

28   **TELLER #2: And he began to be sorrowful and troubled. Then he**
29   **said to them, "My soul is overwhelmed with sorrow to the**
30   **point of death"** (Matthew 26:37-38).

31   **TELLER #1: He was oppressed and afflicted, yet he did not open**
32   **his mouth** (Isaiah 53:7).

33   **TELLER #2: When he was accused by the chief priests and the**
34   **elders, he gave no answer** (Matthew 27:12).

35   **TELLER #1: For he bore the sin of many, and made intercession**

1   for the transgressors (Isaiah 53:12).

2   TELLER #2: **When they came to the place called the Skull, there**

3   **they crucified him, along with the criminals — one on his**

4   **right, the other on his left. Jesus said, "Father, forgive them,**

5   **for they do not know what they are doing"** (Luke 23:33-34).

6   TELLER #1: **For he was cut off from the land of the living; for the**

7   **transgressions of my people he was stricken** (Isaiah 53:8).

8   TELLER #2: **When he had received the drink, Jesus said, "It is**

9   **finished." With that, he bowed his head and gave up his spirit**

10   (John 19:30).

11   TELLER #1: **He was assigned a grave with the wicked, and with**

12   **the rich in his death** (Isaiah 53:9).

13   TELLER #2: **As evening approached, there came a rich man from**

14   **Arimathea, named Joseph, who had himself become a disciple**

15   **of Jesus. Going to Pilate, he asked for Jesus' body, and Pilate**

16   **ordered that it be given to him. Joseph took the body,**

17   **wrapped it in a clean linen cloth, and placed it in his own new**

18   **tomb** (Matthew 27:57-60).

19   TELLER #1: *(Toward heaven, as if addressing God)* **You will not**

20   **abandon me to the grave, nor will you let your Holy One see**

21   **decay!** (Psalm 16:10) *(Addressing audience again)* **After the**

22   **suffering of his soul, he will see the light of life** (Isaiah 53:11).

23   TELLER #2: *(With feeling)* **They found the stone rolled away from**

24   **the tomb, but when they entered, they did not find the body of**

25   **the Lord Jesus. While they were wondering about this,**

26   **suddenly two men in clothes that gleamed like lightning stood**

27   **beside them. In their fright the women bowed down with their**

28   **faces to the ground, but the men said to them, "Why do you**

29   **look for the living among the dead? He is not here; he has**

30   **risen!"** (Luke 24:1-6).

31   TELLER #1: *(With feeling, building to a crescendo)* **That is the story!**

32   TELLER #2: **His story!**

33   TELLER #1: **Our story!**

34   TELLER #2: **The story of** *life! (Freeze and blackout, or immediately*

35   *transition to upbeat worship music.)*

The Sheep, the Goats, and Larry

Summary: Larry is settling in for a long afternoon of bowl games. But does his lifestyle reflect the biblical example of compassion or the modern one of complacency?

Purpose: To show that serving Christ means showing compassion to those in need.

Time: 4-6 minutes

Tone: Serious

Cast: Narrator — A skilled and sensitive reader (male or female); Larry — A typical American guy watching TV and snacking (male)

Costume: Dress pants with a shirt and tie

Props/Set: Large bag of chips, bowl, a six-pack of soda, TV, recliner, lamp stand, remote control, a stool for the Narrator

Themes: Addictions, church issues, compassion, consumerism, distractions, modern life, priorities, role models, spiritual health, suffering

Text: "When the Son of Man comes in his glory, and all the angels with him, he will sit on his throne in heavenly glory. All the nations will be gathered before him, and he will separate the people one from another as a shepherd separates the sheep from the goats" (Matthew 25:31-32).

Notes: This sketch contrasts the compassion exhibited in Jesus' story with the complacency exhibited by so many "armchair Christians" today. Once Larry enters, he continues his actions while the Narrator speaks. It's important that the Narrator not pause and wait for him to do the actions, but that he does them as she continues speaking. The text provided is the New Living Translation (NLT). Another translation could be substituted.

1   ***SETTING:*** At home in Larry's family room right before the ball game
2   comes on TV. Larry's chair and TV are at Stage Left. Narrator's
3   stool is at Stage Right. While Narrator recites Matthew 25:31-46,
4   Larry follows the stage directions. As the scene opens, Narrator
5   enters, sits upon the stool and begins telling the story.
6
7   **NARRATOR: But when the Son of Man comes in his glory, and all**
8   **the angels with him, then he will sit upon his glorious throne.**
9   **All the nations will be gathered in his presence, and he will**
10   **separate them as a shepherd separates the sheep from the**
11   **goats. He will place the sheep at his right hand and the goats**
12   **at his left** (Matthew 25:31-33, NLT). *(NARRATOR does not*
13   *pause as LARRY enters. As NARRATOR says "goats at his left,"*
14   *LARRY enters with an armload of chips, sodas, candy bars, and a*
15   *giant bowl. He is ready to settle in for a long afternoon in front of*
16   *the TV. As the NARRATOR continues, he positions himself on the*
17   *chair, kicks off his shoes, and begins to get all the treats ready for*
18   *his couch potato lifestyle.)*
19   **Then the King will say to those on the right, "Come, you**
20   **who are blessed by my Father, inherit the Kingdom prepared**
21   **for you from the foundation of the world. For I was hungry,**
22   **and you fed me"** (Matthew 25:34-35, NLT). *(As NARRATOR*
23   *says "I was hungry," Larry rips open the bag of chips and pours*
24   *them into his bowl. He grabs the remote control and switches on*
25   *the TV. The volume should be adjusted so that it is barely audible*
26   *to the audience beneath the voice of the NARRATOR. As the*
27   *NARRATOR continues, LARRY loosens his tie, unbuttons his*
28   *shirt, and begins to eat the chips.)*
29   **I was thirsty, and you gave me a drink. I was a stranger,**
30   **and you invited me into your home. I was naked, and you gave**
31   **me clothing. I was sick, and you cared for me. I was in prison,**
32   **and you visited me. Then these righteous ones will reply,**
33   **"Lord, when did we ever see you hungry and feed you? Or**
34   **thirsty and give you something to drink? Or a stranger and**
35   **show you hospitality? Or naked and give you clothing? When**

1   did we ever see you sick or in prison, and visit you?" And the
2   King will tell them, "I assure you, when you did it to one of the
3   least of these my brothers and sisters, you were doing it to
4   me!" (Matthew 25:35-40, NLT). *(As NARRATOR says "doing it*
5   *to me," Larry pops open the can of soda and starts guzzling it. He*
6   *feeds his face with the chips. He should be a little sloppy —*
7   *careless without being overly comical. The audience should begin*
8   *to feel the tension between his life and the text being read.)*
9   Then the King will turn to those on the left and say, "Away
10   with you, you cursed ones, into the eternal fire prepared for
11   the Devil and his demons! For I was hungry, and you didn't
12   feed me. I was thirsty, and you didn't give me anything to
13   drink. I was a stranger, and you didn't invite me into your
14   home. I was naked, and you gave me no clothing. I was sick
15   and in prison, and you didn't visit me" (Matthew 25:41-43,
16   NLT). *(LARRY is channel-surfing, snacking, burping, getting*
17   *cozier and cozier.)*
18   Then they will reply, "Lord, when did we ever see you
19   hungry or thirsty or a stranger or naked or sick or in prison,
20   and not help you?" And he will answer, "I assure you, when
21   you refused to help the least of these my brothers and sisters,
22   you were refusing to help me" (Matthew 25:44-45, NLT). *(By*
23   *now, LARRY has become very comfortable, kicking up the footrest*
24   *and leaning back with the bowl of chips on his stomach. He closes*
25   *his eyes ...)*
26   And they will go away into eternal punishment, but the
27   righteous will go into eternal life (Matthew 25:46, NLT). *(As*
28   *NARRATOR says "eternal life," LARRY begins to gently snore.*
29   *NARRATOR stands and exits. Fadeout.)*

God's Top 10 List

Summary: As each commandment is read, Greg and Carol have a ready excuse to show how they don't really break it. Are they right or just blinded by their rationalizations?

Purpose: To show that the Ten Commandments still apply to our lives today.

Time: 8-10 minutes

Tone: Serious with some humorous moments

Cast: Greg — An actor versatile enough to play ten different roles (male); Carol — An actor versatile enough to play ten different roles (female)

Props/Set: Glasses, chairs, coffee mugs, lottery ticket, cross necklace, cell phone

Themes: Church issues, distractions, excuses, guilt, misconceptions about Christianity, modern life, obedience, sin, the Ten Commandments

Text: Exodus 20:1-18 and "Therefore no one will be declared righteous in his sight by observing the law; rather, through the law we become conscious of sin" (Romans 3:20).

Notes: This sketch reveals the excuses people make for breaking the Ten Commandments. It could be used to introduce or summarize a sermon series on the Ten Commandments. Another option is to use excerpts of this sketch for a specific message on one of the Commandments.

1   *SETTING:* Carol and Greg take turns narrating the commandments
2   and delivering brief, contemporary "slice-of-life" monologs that
3   relate to each commandment. Begin with Carol and Greg
4   addressing the audience. When they're reciting the commandments,
5   they directly face the audience. When they deliver the brief
6   monologs, they turn slightly toward each other.
7
8   (Commandment #1)
9   **CAROL:** *(Narrating to audience)* **And God spoke all these words:**
10   (Exodus 20:1)
11   **GREG:** *(Narrating)* **I am the Lord your God, who brought you out**
12   **of Egypt, out of the land of slavery. You shall have no other**
13   **gods before me** (Exodus 20:2-3).
14   **CAROL:** *(As a modern relativist)* **Well, that may be true for you, but**
15   **it's not true for me. I just can't accept that there's only one**
16   **way to heaven. That's such a narrow, intolerant view! I try to**
17   **be more inclusive and open-minded. I'm a very spiritual**
18   **person, but I'm not committed to any one religion in**
19   **particular. I've taken the best that each religion has to offer**
20   **and created my own set of beliefs.**
21   **GREG:** *(As a modern moralist)* **I try to live a good life, you know. I**
22   **go to church, I don't get drunk or do drugs or cheat on my**
23   **wife. I teach my children that religion is an important part of**
24   **developing healthy values. But I'll leave it up to them to**
25   **decide what religion to choose. I wouldn't want to force my**
26   **views on them. Yeah … I like to think of myself as a Christian,**
27   **in all the best sense of the word.**
28
29   (Commandment #2)
30   **CAROL: You shall not make for yourself an idol in the form of**
31   **anything in heaven above or on the earth beneath or in the**
32   **waters below** (Exodus 20:4).
33   **GREG:** *(Pulling a cross necklace out from under his shirt)* **Why do I**
34   **wear this cross? You know, to represent what Jesus did. It's a**
35   **symbol of my faith. I never take it off — not because I'm**

1 superstitious or anything, just because I don't want to
2 compromise my views. I think any church that doesn't have a
3 cross up front couldn't really be a Bible-believing church. *(He*
4 *tucks the cross back in his shirt.)*
5 CAROL: *(As a contemporary super-mom)* I was helping out in
6 Matt's third-grade class last week, and they were studying
7 African culture. Each class made these cute little cardboard
8 village gods out of paper towel rolls. Then they decorated
9 them with ribbons and streamers and sang some traditional
10 tribal songs. I just think it's great that they're studying the
11 traditions and practices of other cultures!
12
13 (Commandment #3)
14 GREG: You shall not misuse the name of the Lord your God, for
15 the Lord will not hold anyone guiltless who misuses his name
16 (Exodus 20:7).
17 CAROL: *(She is scratching a lottery ticket.)* Oh, my God! Oh, my
18 God! I won! I can't believe it! Look at this! I won! Oh, my
19 God! Oh, am I on TV? Oh, my God! Oh, my God! I can't
20 believe it! *(Alternate line: [CAROL pretends to speak on the*
21 *phone.] Can you believe it? Alan likes you! Yeah! I'm not kidding!*
22 *It's true. Lacey told me! I swear to God! Isn't that awesome?)*
23 GREG: *(Sitting down and dramatically folding hands for a meal*
24 *prayer. These lines are delivered very rhythmically and quickly,*
25 *with no pause after the prayer.)* Come, Lord Jesus, be our guest,
26 and let these gifts to us be blessed. Amen. Pass the potatoes,
27 would you please, dear? Let's dig in! I just love roast beef. So
28 what'd you learn at school today, kids?
29
30 (Commandment #4)
31 CAROL: Remember the Sabbath day by keeping it holy. Six days
32 you shall labor and do all your work, but the seventh day is a
33 Sabbath to the Lord your God (Exodus 20:8-10).
34 GREG: *(Complaining)* I just didn't get anything out of that sermon
35 today. I mean, the preacher just went on and on and on. I

1   finally figured out the pattern for every sermon he does: Guilt
2   trip, guilt trip, guilt trip, but God loves you anyway. Amen.
3   And the choir was off-key ... The doughnuts were stale ... I
4   found three typos in the bulletin ... They used that old-
5   fashioned translation of the Bible ... And nobody greeted us
6   when we walked in. What a waste of time. We should find a
7   church where they take worshiping God a little more
8   seriously.
9   CAROL: *(Miming driving a car, holding a cell phone to her ear with*
10   *her shoulder)* **Honey, I know what day it is, but I haven't sold**
11   a house in two months, and the Beckers can only see the house
12   today. I really think they're ready to buy. It'll only take a
13   couple hours for me to show them the house. Yeah, OK, I'll see
14   you tonight. 'Bye.
15
16   (Commandment #5)
17   GREG: Honor your father and your mother, so that you may live
18   long in the land the Lord your God is giving you (Exodus
19   20:12).
20   CAROL: Well, I'm not trying to be cruel or anything, but there just
21   isn't room here for your mother! I mean, we're cramped in
22   this tiny apartment the way it is, and besides, we've got our
23   own kids to take care of. I can't be spending all my time caring
24   for your mom ... I really think the nursing home is the best
25   place for her. We'll visit her. Don't worry. Really. It's best for
26   everyone.
27   GREG: Hey, listen, my old man is a loser and a drunk. And there's
28   no way I'm gonna fly halfway across the country just because
29   his liver finally gave out. He's been drinking himself to death
30   for years. And he was never there for me. Why should I go out
31   of my way for him? I'll send him a card or something.
32
33   (Commandment #6)
34   CAROL: You shall not murder (Exodus 20:13).
35   GREG: *(Pretending to be driving, speaking to an imaginary*

1 *passenger)* **So anyway, I'm walking up to the water cooler,**
2 **right? And Davis comes over to me, and he starts talking**
3 **about how he should have gotten last month's sales award**
4 **instead of me and —** *(To an unseen driver)* **Hey! Hey, buddy!**
5 **What do you think you're doing? You jerk!** *(To his passenger)*
6 **Did you see that? That guy just pulled right in front of me! I**
7 **hate those people who think the road belongs to them!** *(To*
8 *unseen driver)* **Jerk! I wish you'd drop dead, you road hog!**
9 CAROL: **I couldn't believe it when I got the news. I mean, the**
10 **timing could not have been worse. Joe was still in graduate**
11 **school, and I was working like sixty hours a week just to help**
12 **pay the bills. I mean, don't get me wrong, we want to have**
13 **kids. Just not yet … So I got it taken care of. I mean, what**
14 **would you expect me to do? I never even told Joe. Every child**
15 **should be a wanted child, not one that disrupts your life.**
16 **Right? You know? You understand what I'm saying, don't**
17 **you?**
18
19 (Commandment #7)
20 **GREG: You shall not commit adultery** (Exodus 20:14).
21 CAROL: *(Pretending to be talking to a friend)* **Well, we were going**
22 **through a really rough time in our marriage, OK? Eric never**
23 **listened to me anymore, and he spent all his extra time at the**
24 **health club or at work. And then, when Dylan came along, he**
25 **just made me feel so special. I felt young again. Loved. You**
26 **can't knock me for wanting that, can you? Just wanting to feel**
27 **loved?**
28 GREG: **I travel a lot, you know. It can get lonely on the road. So I**
29 **hang out at the gentlemen's clubs, and it's no big deal. My**
30 **wife knows about it. It's not like I'm cheating on her or**
31 **anything. I just look. I don't touch. That way everyone's**
32 **happy.**
33
34 (Commandment #8)
35 **CAROL: You shall not steal** (Exodus 20:15).

1 GREG: Hey, anytime you need some more carpentry work done,
2   give me a call. I like working for you guys, 'cause you always
3   pay me cash up front. That way Uncle Sam can keep his
4   grubby little fingers out of my pocket. Know what I mean? He
5   gets enough of my hard-earned cash the way it is!
6 CAROL: *(Going through her pockets)* Uh, I'm all out of change.
7   Why don't you just order one of those drinks with the free
8   refills, and we can just take turns using the same cup? They
9   overprice their drinks here anyway.
10
11 (Commandment #9)
12 GREG: You shall not give false testimony against your neighbor
13   (Exodus 20:16).
14 CAROL: *(Pretending to be sincerely admiring another woman's outfit)*
15   Oh, that dress is just you! I mean, it really brings out ... the
16   highlights in your hair! It's so ... indescribable. It's not a
17   design that you see every day! I just can't imagine anyone else
18   looking any better in it!
19 GREG: *(Leaning through an imaginary doorway)* Miss Lawson, I'm
20   gonna be in my office all afternoon finishing up the Lewis
21   proposal, so if anyone calls, just tell them I stepped out of the
22   building or something.
23
24 (Commandment #10)
25 CAROL: You shall not covet ... anything that belongs to your
26   neighbor (Exodus 20:17).
27 GREG: *(As a disgruntled businessman)* I can't believe they passed
28   me up for the promotion! I've been working at that stupid
29   place three years longer than Bill Parrish has! And now he's
30   driving that Lexus just to spite me. I'll probably be driving
31   this Buick until I retire.
32 CAROL: *(Seated, drinking coffee)* I just wish I had more time away
33   from the kids, that's all. It's not like I'm Karen Wilson or
34   anything. I mean, her parents take her kids every other
35   weekend! She and Neal went to this cute little bed and

1   breakfast last month, and she hasn't stopped talking about it.
2   It's just not fair that we don't have any family in the area!
3   **GREG:**   *(To audience)* When the people saw the thunder and
4   lightning and heard the trumpet and saw the mountain in
5   smoke, they trembled with fear. They stayed at a distance
6   (Exodus 20:18).
7   **CAROL:**   The Ten Commandments? Are you kidding? What do
8   they have to do with life today? I mean, they're awfully old-
9   fashioned, don't you think? *(Freeze. Fadeout.)*
10
11
12
13
14
15
16
17
18
19
20
21
22
23
24
25
26
27
28
29
30
31
32
33
34
35

Talking to God

Summary: Mandy and Jordan demonstrate a variety of prayers.

Purpose: To demonstrate both genuine and insincere ways of praying to get people thinking about how they address God.

Time: 5-7 minutes

Tone: Serious with lighthearted moments

Cast: Mandy — An actor able to be both serious and humorous (female); Jordan — An actor able to be both serious and humorous (male)

Props/Set: Baseball hat, papers, stack of envelopes, chair, table

Themes: Appearances, authenticity, church issues, faith, Jesus, listening, prayer, repentance, second chances, spiritual health

Text: Luke 18:9-14 (The Two Praying Men) and "But when you pray, go into your room, close the door and pray to your Father, who is unseen. Then your Father, who sees what is done in secret, will reward you. And when you pray, do not keep on babbling like pagans, for they think they will be heard because of their many words" (Matthew 6:6-7).

Notes: After each "prayer," Jordan turns his back to the audience and freezes while Mandy delivers her lines. She does the same. You may wish to have background music for some or all of the prayers. Be careful so that you aren't mocking people who pray differently than you, just that you are showing a variety of prayers and letting people see the genuineness or artificiality of each.

1 **SETTING:** Mandy and Jordan will portray a variety of characters in
2 this sketch. The setting for each mini-monolog is different.
3
4 **MANDY:** *(Turning to face the audience, kneeling and folding hands,*
5 *speaking rhythmically and unemotionally)* **Now I lay me down to**
6 **sleep, I pray the Lord my soul to keep. If I should die before**
7 **I wake, I pray the Lord my soul to take. If I should live**
8 **another day, I pray the Lord would guide my way. Amen.**
9 *(Stands, turns her back to the audience, and freezes.)*
10 **JORDAN:** *(Turning to face the audience, genuinely confessing to God)*
11 **Hey, God. It's me again. I know I just talked to you this**
12 **morning but, well, I did it again. I know I promised you I**
13 **wouldn't do it. I know. I know. I'm sorry. It's just so**
14 **addicting. Forgive me. Please, God, forgive me.** *(Turns with*
15 *back to the audience and freezes.)*
16 **MANDY:** *(Turns to face the audience. She is seated and is collating*
17 *envelopes, putting a letter in each one, and then sealing it shut.*
18 *As she rhythmically works, she quietly begins whistling "Amazing*
19 *Grace." Take your time with this. Don't rush it. Let the audience*
20 *realize it's a nonverbal prayer. As she finishes whistling, she*
21 *smiles and freezes, then stands and turns her back to the*
22 *audience.)*
23 **JORDAN:** *(Turning to face the audience, enthusiastically)* **Good food,**
24 **good meat, good God, let's eat!** *(Turns with back to the audience*
25 *and freezes.)*
26 **MANDY:** *(Facing audience, very "religiously," making the sign of a*
27 *cross, chanting like a monk)* **Our Father who art in heaven,**
28 **hallowed by thy name. Thy kingdom come, thy will be done**
29 **on earth as it is in heaven. Give us this day our daily bread.**
30 **And forgive us our trespasses as we forgive those who trespass**
31 **against us. And lead us not into temptation, but deliver us**
32 **from evil.** *(Makes the sign of the cross, then turns and freezes.)*
33 **JORDAN:** *(Facing audience, pretending to be golfing)* **C'mon, God.**
34 **If you just let me make this putt, I promise I'll go back to**
35 **church. I'll stop swearing and drinking, and I'll read my**

1   Bible every day. I promise. I'll give up meat. I'll shave my

2   head. Anything you want, just please, let me make this putt ...

3   *(Turns and freezes.)*

4   **MANDY:** *(Facing audience, intensely)* God! It's not fair! Don't take

5   my baby! Don't take my baby, God! God? Are you listening to

6   me? Don't take my baby away! *(Turns and freezes.)*

7   **JORDAN:** *(Facing audience, raising hands above his head,*

8   *emphasizing the word "just")* I just ask that you just bless

9   Justin and just help him and just be with him. And I just

10   thank you for just being God and for just helping me with just

11   everything. You're just, you're just, you're just so ... just. It's

12   just cool. *(Turns and freezes.)*

13 **MANDY:** *(Facing audience)* Oh, God, I'd really like to find a

14   husband. If it's your will, send me a man who's about six-two,

15   one hundred and eighty-five pounds, likes kids, plays tennis,

16   has a nice steady job with a good insurance policy, doesn't

17   snore, and loves taking his wife to antique stores on the

18   weekends. If it's your will, let him be named Aaron and let

19   him get a divorce from Julia as soon as possible ... but only if

20   it's your will, God. *(Turns and freezes.)*

21 **JORDAN:** *(Facing audience, putting on a baseball cap backward, as*

22   *a child)* Dear God, please bless *(Quickly)* Grandma and

23   Grandpa, Grams and Gramps, Auntie Jo and Uncle Fred,

24   Mommy, Daddy, Susie, and my puppy Bingo. Thanks for

25   sunshine and ice cream and belly buttons and baseball. And

26   please forgive me for the whole gerbil incident. I really

27   thought with the wings I duct-taped on him, he'd be able to

28   make it from the tree house back to my window ... Oh, and

29   thanks for the vet and that little plastic cast. I love you, God.

30   Amen. *(Turns and freezes.)*

31 **MANDY:** *(Facing audience, humbly)* God, I don't really know how

32   to do this. I guess it's the first time we've ever really spoken.

33   My friend said that if I'd trust in you, you'd rescue me from

34   my past and my sins and my failures. That you'd give me a

35   future. That you really love me. So here I am, Jesus. I want

1   you to be my Savior. I need you. **Take my sins away, and give**
2   **me your peace instead ...** *(Miming bowing her head, placing her*
3   *head in her hands, raising one hand affectionately, praying*
4   *silently for a moment, then standing, wiping tears from her eyes,*
5   *smiling, turning her back to audience, and freezing)*
6   **JORDAN:** *(Facing audience)* **Dearest Father God, thanks for the**
7   **new job and all those great benefits. I know it had to come**
8   **from you, God. I just thank you for the house and the cars and**
9   **the boat and all the great things you've given me. I thank you**
10   **that I'm able to tithe and give you back a portion of what**
11   **you've given to me. And I thank you that I'm not involved in**
12   **any shady business deals and that I'm not struggling with**
13   **lust, swearing, or gossiping, like Mark. Thanks that I don't**
14   **have a drug habit to support, like Bruce — I'm sure glad I'm**
15   **not in his shoes. I just thank you that I'm an overall nice guy**
16   **... that everybody likes me, and** *(Pausing as he realizes this)*
17   **that I really don't need you all that much, now that I think**
18   **about it. Amen.** *(Turns and freezes. Both now have backs to*
19   *audience. Fadeout.)*
20
21
22
23
24
25
26
27
28
29
30
31
32
33
34
35

Released! Released!

Summary: Two storytellers recite a rhyming summary of Jesus' life and mission.

Purpose: To show that Christ came to set us free from fear, sin, and death.

Time: 3-5 minutes

Tone: Worshipful

Cast: Teller #1 — (male or female); Teller #2 — (male or female)

Costumes: Black turtlenecks and blue jeans (or another neutral outfit) for the tellers

Props/Set: None

Themes: Christmas, Easter, faith, forgiveness, God's power, Jesus, new life

Text: Various

Notes: This dramatic presentation of images from the life of Jesus could be a very powerful and emotional addition to a special Christmas or Easter program. The tellers are dressed in neutral colors or all black. If desired, choreograph their movements to match their words. If available, use background music for all or part of this sketch.

1   *SETTING:* The stage is bare.

2

3   TELLER #1: **Alone. Afraid. A journey made.**

4   TELLER #2: **A night. A plight. A barn. A babe.**

5   TELLER #1: **Angels.**

6   TELLER #2: **Shepherds.**

7   TELLER #1: **Worship.**

8   TELLER #2: **Praise.**

9   TELLER #1: **Wise men. Gifts.**

10   TELLER #2: **Egyptian ways.**

11   TELLER #1: **Back home. Now grown. Who is this man?**

12   TELLER #2: **Baptized and tempted. Walked the land.**

13   TELLER #1: **Stood tall.**

14   TELLER #2: **Obeyed.**

15   TELLER #1: **Cared and sought.**

16   TELLER #2: **Led and healed.**

17   TELLER #1: **Preached**

18   TELLER #2: **And taught.**

19   TELLER #1: **Disciples. Questions. Prayers and song.**

20   TELLER #2: **Teachers. Doubting. Acting strong.**

21   TELLER #1: **A colt.**

22   TELLER #2: **Procession.**

23   TELLER #1: **Plots**

24   TELLER #2: **And schemes.**

25   TELLER #1: **Judas. Silver.**

26   TELLER #2: **Garden dreams.**

27   TELLER #1: **Prayer.**

28   TELLER #2: **Torches.**

29   TELLER #1: **A kiss.**

30   TOGETHER: **Betrayed!**

31   TELLER #2: **One man alone, yet unafraid.**

32   TELLER #1: **A trial.**

33   TELLER #2: **Questions.**

34   TELLER #1: **No reply.**

35   TELLER #2: **High Priest.**

1   TELLER #1: "Guilty!"
2   TELLER #2: Rooster's cry.
3   TELLER #1: Pilate.
4   TELLER #2: Herod.
5   TELLER #1: Pilate again.
6   TELLER #2: No guilt at all.
7   TELLER #1: No guilt?
8   TELLER #2: But then —
9   TELLER #1: Beatings. Thorns. A screaming crowd.
10   TELLER #2: "Release Barabbas!"
11   TELLER #1: Request allowed.
12   TELLER #2: A cross. A road. Outside of town.
13   TELLER #1: Guilt and shame that weighed him down.
14   TELLER #2: Forsaken.
15   TELLER #1: Dying.
16   TELLER #2: Hopeless will.
17   TELLER #1: Thieves.
18   TELLER #2: Darkness.
19   TELLER #1: Quiet.
20   TOGETHER: Still.
21   TELLER #2: "Dead?"
22   TELLER #1: Confirmed — no broken bone.
23   TELLER #2: Another's tomb. A giant stone.
24   TELLER #1: Buried. Sealed. Entrance barred.
25   TELLER #2: Waiting. Watching. Under guard.
26   TELLER #1: Sunday.
27   TELLER #2: Empty?!
28   TELLER #1: An angel white!
29   TELLER #2: Surprise. Confusion … and delight!
30   TELLER #1: Women.
31   TELLER #2: Running!
32   TELLER #1: The news!
33   TELLER #2: The doubt —
34   TELLER #1: Peter and John.
35   TELLER #2: The word is out.

1   TELLER #1: A road. Afraid. A visit paid.
2   TELLER #2: Two friends depressed. A third. Amazed!
3   TELLER #1: A sealed room within closed doors
4   TELLER #2: And then ... their Friend! His hands. The sores!
5   TELLER #1: Now, hope!
6   TELLER #2: Now, life!
7   TELLER #1: A promise made.
8   TELLER #2: No more alone!
9   TELLER #1: "Be not afraid."
10   TELLER #2: The Way!
11   TELLER #1: The Truth!
12   TELLER #2: The Life
13   TELLER #1: And peace!
14   TELLER #2: Eternal rest.
15   TELLER #1: Released! Released! *(Freeze and blackout, or*
16   *immediately transition to upbeat worship music.)*
17
18
19
20
21
22
23
24
25
26
27
28
29
30
31
32
33
34
35

Theme Index

235

Verse Index

Cast Index

One Man, One Woman

Two Men

Two Women

Either Men or Women

© 2001 Eric McCarty/The Light Photography

About the Author

Steven James is an award-winning writer and professional storyteller. He completed his Master of Arts in Storytelling in 1997. Since then, he has shared his unique blend of storytelling, drama, and comedy through his approximately 300 speaking engagements yearly at conferences, retreats, and churches across the country.

In addition, he has trained thousands of actors, speakers and educators worldwide on creative communication and effective storytelling techniques. He is actively involved in his home church as director of its drama ministry.

In 1999, Steven was honored as "Writer of the Year" at the American Christian Writers' Conference. Over 200 of his articles and scripts have appeared in dozens of Christian and inspirational media, such as *A Second Helping of Chicken Soup for the Woman's Soul, Guideposts 4 Teens, With,* and many others. This is his second book.

When Steven is not writing or performing, he likes canoeing, watching science fiction movies, and eating chicken fajitas (although not usually at the same time).

Steven lives with his wife, Liesl, and their three daughters, Trinity, Ariel, and Eden, in Tennessee.

Steven James' Website: http://www.nextgennow.com/

Order Form

Meriwether Publishing Ltd.
PO Box 7710
Colorado Springs CO 80933-7710
Phone: 800-937-5297 Fax: 719-594-9916
Website: www.meriwether.com

Please send me the following books:

_____ **Worship Sketches 2 Perform #BK-B242** $15.95
by Steven James
A collection of scripts for two actors

_____ **More Worship Sketches 2 Perform #BK-B258** $14.95
by Steven James
A collection of scripts for two actors

_____ **Service with a Smile #BK-B225** $14.95
by Daniel Wray
52 humorous sketches for Sunday worship

_____ **Isaac Air Freight: The Works 2 #BK-B243** $16.95
by Dan Rupple and Dave Toole
More sketches from the premier Christian comedy group

_____ **Isaac Air Freight: The Works #BK-B215** $16.95
by Dan Rupple and Dave Toole
Sketches from the premier Christian comedy group

_____ **Divine Comedies #BK-B190** $12.95
by T. M. Williams
A collection of plays for church drama groups

_____ **Sermons Alive! #BK-B132** $14.95
by Paul Neale Lessard
52 dramatic sketches for worship services

These and other fine Meriwether Publishing books are available at
your local bookstore or direct from the publisher. Prices subject to
change without notice. Check our website or call for current prices.

Name: _____

Organization name: _____

Address: _____

City: _____ State: _____

Zip: _____ Phone: _____

❑ **Check enclosed**

❑ **Visa / MasterCard / Discover #** _____

Signature: _____   *Expiration date:* _____

(required for credit card orders)

Colorado residents: Please add 3% sales tax.
Shipping: Include $4.95 for the first book and 75¢ for each additional book ordered.

❑ *Please send me a copy of your complete catalog of books and plays.*